THE WAY OF NATURE

THE ILLUSTRATED LIBRARY OF CHINESE CLASSICS

The Illustrated Library of Chinese Classics brings together a series of immensely appealing and popular graphic narratives about traditional Asian philosophy and literature, all written and illustrated by C. C. Tsai, one of East Asia's most beloved cartoonists. Playful, humorous, and genuinely illuminating, these unique adaptations offer ideal introductions to the most influential writers, works, and schools of ancient Chinese thought and beyond.

The Analects • Confucius

The Art of War • Sunzi

Zhuangzi

THE WAY OF NATURE

Adapted and illustrated by

C. C. Tsai

Translated by Brian Bruya

Foreword by Edward Slingerland

Copyright © 2019 by Princeton University Press

Published by Princeton University Press
41 William Street, Princeton, New Jersey 08540
6 Oxford Street, Woodstock, Oxfordshire OX20 1TR

press.princeton.edu

All Rights Reserved

Library of Congress Control Number: 2018958696
ISBN (pbk.) 978-0-691-17974-2

British Library Cataloging-in-Publication Data is available

Editorial: Rob Tempio and Matt Rohal
Production Editorial: Mark Bellis
Text Design: C. Alvarez-Gaffin
Lettering: Meghan Kanabay
Cover Design: Michael Boland for thebolanddesignco.com
Cover Image Credit: C. C. Tsai
Production: Erin Suydam
Publicity: Jodi Price and Katie Lewis
Copyeditor: Shanti Fader Whitesides

This book has been composed in News Gothic and Adobe Fangsong

Printed on acid-free paper. ∞

Printed in the United States of America

10 9 8 7 6 5 4 3 2

Contents

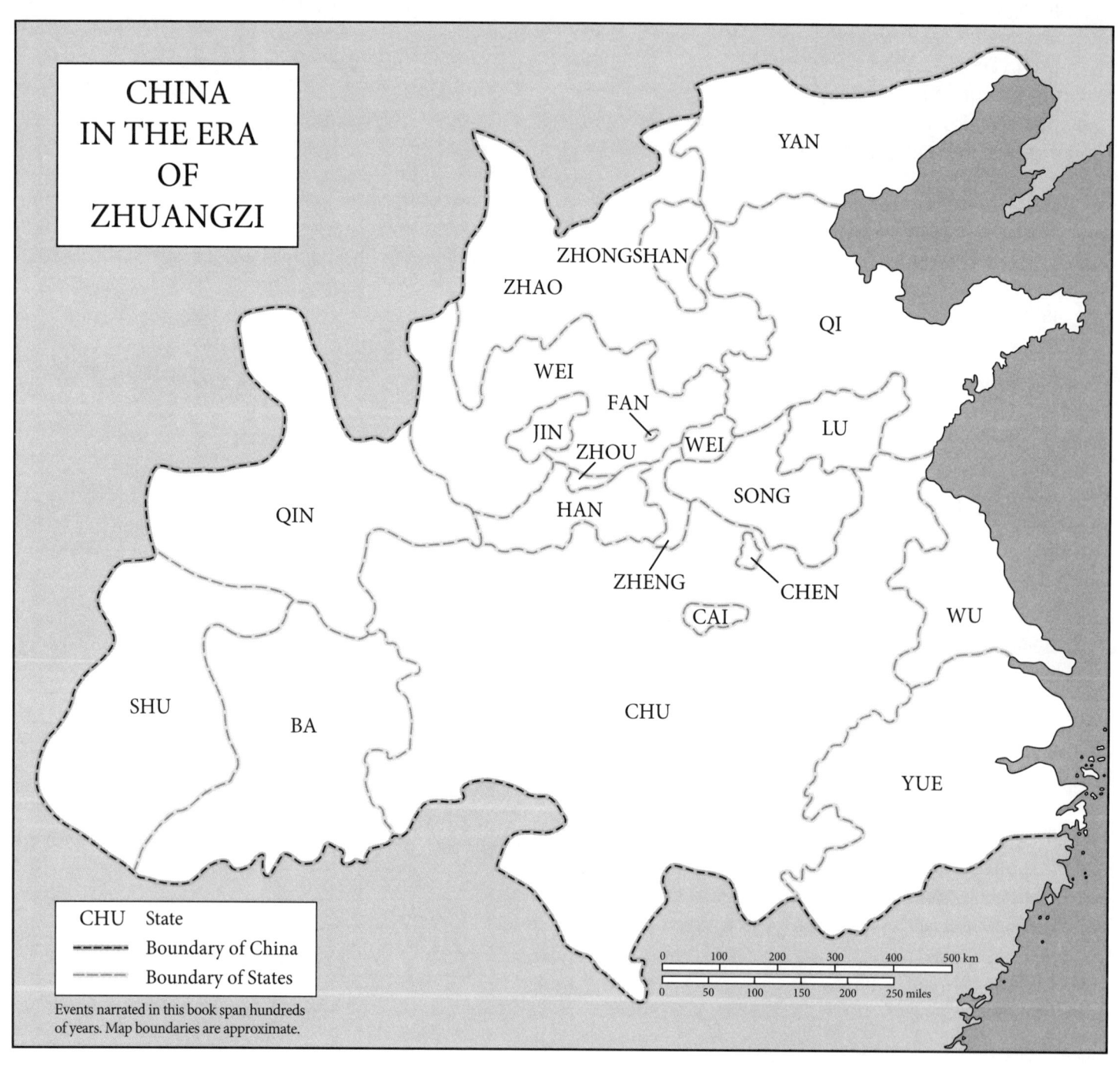

CHINA
IN THE ERA
OF
ZHUANGZI

YAN

ZHONGSHAN

ZHAO

QI

WEI

FAN

JIN

ZHOU

WEI

LU

HAN

SONG

ZHENG

CHEN

CAI

WU

QIN

SHU

BA

CHU

YUE

CHU   State

- - - -   Boundary of China

- - - -   Boundary of States

Events narrated in this book span hundreds
of years. Map boundaries are approximate.

0   100   200   300   400   500 km

0   50   100   150   200   250 miles

Foreword

EDWARD SLINGERLAND

As a student of classical Chinese in Taiwan in the late 1980s, I was asked by my tutors what texts I was interested in reading. My answer was definitive and singular: the *Zhuangzi*. Having encountered this mind-bending, life-changing text through the English-language renderings of Thomas Merton, and then Burton Watson's translation, the *Zhuangzi* was the reason I had chosen to study classical Chinese, and I was eager to begin engaging with it in the original.

It turned out to be a lot harder than I thought. The *Zhuangzi* is stylistically and conceptually unlike any other Warring States (5th–3rd century BCE) text. The brilliance of its author(s)—let's call him, her, or them "Zhuangzi" for the sake of convenience—is reflected in its distinctive and challenging language. Dissatisfied with the expressive possibilities of the classical Chinese on offer at the time, Zhuangzi created a wild array of new adjectives and adverbs, many of them onomatopoetic, that early Chinese commentators on the text struggled to explain. The concepts and characters are even crazier. Logical paradoxes, enormous mythical fish that turn into giant birds and fly south, people's organs being transformed into owls—I had chosen probably the worst possible text, in terms of easy comprehensibility, for my initiation into classical Chinese.

Somewhat discouraged by my slow progress, I was surprised to spot an intriguing-looking comic book in one of the local bookstores—an illustrated version of the *Zhuangzi* by C. C. Tsai. The drawings themselves were wonderful and really seemed to capture the spirit of the text as I'd glimpsed it in English. Probably more importantly, the *baihua* (colloquial) Chinese explanations and dialogues vividly brought to life the conversations and stories that I was struggling to comprehend as I slogged through the painfully difficult original text. The original classical Chinese appeared in the margins, so I could refer back to it, but the illustrations and lively modern Chinese gave me an easy and pleasurable way to access the ideas behind the text.

I remember thinking that, after returning to the States, I would one day translate Tsai's works into English to make them available to a wider audience. Brian Bruya beat me to it, and I'm really glad he did. The colloquial Chinese translations that Tsai puts into the mouths of his characters are very tricky to render into smooth and accessible English, but Bruya handles this challenge perfectly. It would be impossible to do better than Nie Que's "Sheesh! What a letdown . . . ," when confronted with Wang Ni's lack of knowledge ("Does Wang Ni Know?"), or the annoyed crow muttering, "Gimme a break," when different species of birds ardently debate which color is best in "Crows and Seagulls." Bruya's translation is effortless, accurate, and a pleasure to read.

And read it you should. The *Zhuangzi* is probably the most overlooked great work of world literature. It is one of the two foundational texts of a school of thought subsequently referred to as "Daoism," along with the *Daodejing* traditionally (and almost certainly apocryphally) attributed to Laozi, or the "Old Master." There are good reasons why early imperial librarians classed these two books together. Both see civilization, and Confucian culture in particular, as somehow antithetic to our true nature. Both view language with suspicion, as something that limits our worldview. And both have a basic faith in human beings' innate, untutored nature.

I would argue that the *Zhuangzi*, however, has a much more sophisticated answer to the question of how human beings should live. Laozi urges us to get rid of learning and culture, and physically return to a primitive, utopian life of small-scale agriculture. Zhuangzi sees us as already embedded in, and inextricably tied to, civilized life. Humans will continue to write and read books, carve bell-stands and perform social rituals, argue with one another and travel to faraway lands. The key is to do this without losing your connection with Heaven, the natural force that governs the world and created our natures. One should live like the clever birds in the "Swallows Nest in the Eaves" story, being "in the world but not of it," to borrow language from the New Testament. The way to do this is to make one's mind tenuous or empty, open to the true nature of the world and people around you, so that you go along with things rather than striving to impose your will or preconceived notions on them.

The insights of the *Zhuangzi* have much to teach us today. Over the last fifteen years or so I've grown increasingly involved in various branches of the cognitive sciences. The more I learn about the nature of human cognition, the more prescient the insights of the *Zhuangzi* seem to me. The story of "Huizi's Giant Gourds," for instance, tells of Zhuangzi's logician friend Hui Shi (Huizi), who smashes some giant gourds because they are too big to be used as ladles and too shallow to use as bowls. To get the point of the story it is important to realize that these are the two standard uses of a gourd in early China: when Hui Shi hears the word "gourd," he immediately thinks of either ladles or bowls. This is a good example of what psychologists call "categorical inflexibility," where standard definitions or images associated with certain words limit our cognitive fluidity.

The importance of thinking flexibly, outside the cage of conventional categories, is also the point of the various "usefulness of the useless" stories, like that of "The Useless *Shu* Tree" or "The Earth Spirit's Tree."

Similarly, the story of the monkey trainer and the chestnuts in "Three at Dawn and Four at Dusk" makes an important point about the power of psychological framing: the same facts can inspire very different emotional reactions, as well as consequent behaviors, depending upon how they are characterized. Vastly more people favor a treatment proposed for a hypothetical disease said to be affecting six hundred people when the outcome is described as "two hundred lives saved" rather than "four hundred will die." A wise person will use this knowledge to nudge others in the right direction. "The Cook Carves Up a Cow" and "The Old Wheelwright," examples of the famous "skill stories" in the *Zhuangzi*, get at the power of embodied cognition, while "Learning How to Walk in Handan" vividly illustrates the interference of cognitive control in skillful action, a central theme of the literature on choking in sports and performance. "The Caged Pheasant" hints at the danger of the hedonic treadmill—the fact that humans are built to never be satisfied by current pleasures—while "The Horse Lover" points to the danger of suffocating attachments.

All of these stories are designed to teach us how to move skillfully and flexibly through the world, engaging genuinely with what comes and living out our ordained lifespans with equanimity and grace. I hope readers will enjoy this book as much as I do.

Introduction

BRIAN BRUYA

I. THE BATTLE OF THE HUNDRED SCHOOLS

The Imperial Period in China began in 221 BCE, when the First Emperor, hailing from the far western state of Qin, completed his conquest of China. From that time until 1911, there were six subsequent major dynasties: the Han, Tang, Song, Yuan, Ming, and Qing. But what about before the Qin? For 789 years, from 1045 to 256 BCE (much longer than any subsequent dynasty), a single lineage held the throne as Son of Heaven, ruler of China. This dynasty's name is Zhou (pronounced joe—see the Pronunciation Index in the back of the book for how to pronounce other Chinese names and terms). The period of the Zhou that concerns us is the second half, when traditional order had broken down.

The traditional order was unique among world civilizations. The Zhou Dynasty begins with the victors over the preceding Shang Dynasty fanning out across the country, taking control of key cities and towns—over 150 in total. We can think of each of these newly formed states as a fief, loyal to the Zhou king. Each enfeoffed ruler had local control but served at the pleasure of the king: visiting the king regularly to renew bonds of fealty, sending tribute to the king, and doing the king's bidding when necessary. Each fief was handed down to the ruler's eldest son. In the beginning, these fiefs were close, either in terms of familial relationships or in terms of military loyalty, and the relationship between king and vassal was viewed as like that between father and son. Over time, however, disputes arose, loyalties frayed, and battles occurred. 250 years in, and ties were stretched to the breaking point.

A traditional story (perhaps apocryphal) is often used to illustrate a key turning point in the dynasty. In 773 BCE, the king had just divorced his primary wife and replaced her with his favorite, who was difficult to please. In order to entertain her, the king arranged for a large feast on the outskirts of the capital, and at nightfall he had the warning beacons on the city wall lit. The beacons went up in flame one after another in a spectacular display that reached to the horizon, and, after several hours, troops from neighboring states arrived breathless at the capital to bring aid to the king, whom they thought was in grave danger from invasion. The spectacle delighted the queen, but of course the generals and soldiers who had rushed to help were not amused. This happened more than once.

Not long after, the state of Shen, which nursed a grudge against the king, allied with the Quan Rong tribe and attacked the Zhou capital. When the Zhou warning beacons were lit, the neighboring states ignored them. The capital was laid waste, and the king was killed. The Zhou lineage was allowed to continue, but it was forced to move its capital east, its area of direct control was reduced, and it lost the fealty of the major vassals. From that point on, the various states quickly realized it was every state for itself. For the next five and a half centuries the states gradually swallowed each other up until only seven major states remained at the end of the Spring & Autumn Period (770–481 BCE). As armies increased in size during the Warring States Period (481–221 BCE), the disruption of warfare increased as well. The battle for ultimate supremacy continued until Qin was the last state standing.

In this battle for ultimate supremacy it would no longer do for a ruler to simply rely on his circle of close nobility to act as generals and ministers. Every ruler needed the most capable people around. And so an intellectual ferment began. Not only did rulers look beyond the nobility for brains and talent but people of brains and talent began to promote their own views about how best to govern—theories that blossomed to include all kinds of associated philosophical concerns. Over time, similar lines of thinking coalesced into a variety of schools of thought, such as Confucianism, Mo-ism, Legalism, Daoism, and so on. The Chinese refer to it as the period of the contending voices of a hundred schools of thought.

The first major Confucian thinker was Confucius, represented in the *Analects* of Confucius, a handbook for creating a flourishing society through cultural education and strong moral leadership. Mencius, a student of Confucius's grandson, Zisi, was the second major Confucian thinker. His influential book, the *Mencius*, uses memorable analogies and thought experiments (such as the child on the edge of a well) to drive home subtle points about the goodness of human nature and effective governing. Two short pieces that were important to the revival of Confucianism in the Song Dynasty were also products of this time. They are *Advanced Education* (*Da Xue*) and *The Middle Path* (*Zhong Yong*), traditionally attributed to Confucius' student Zengzi and to Zisi, respectively. *Advanced Education* offers a pithy formula for the self-development of caring, world-class leaders, and *The Middle Path* discusses how to achieve balance both internally and externally.

While the Confucians concentrated on creating moral leaders, others, known to us now as Daoists, preferred to concentrate on becoming as close as possible to the natural way of things. The major Daoist texts from this period are the *Zhuangzi* and Laozi's *Daodejing*. The *Zhuangzi* is one of the great works of world literature, simultaneously a profound philosophical study of metaphysics, language, epistemology, and ethics. It's also seriously fun to read for its colorful characters and paradoxical stories. Laozi's *Daodejing* echoes many themes of the *Zhuangzi*, with an emphasis on the sage as leader, non-action, and emptying the mind. Its poetic language and spare style

stand it in stark contrast to the *Zhuangzi* but also allow for a richness of interpretation that has made it an all-time favorite of contemplative thinkers across traditions. A third Daoist from this time period, Liezi, had his name placed on a book a few centuries later. The *Liezi* adopts the style and themes of the *Zhuangzi* and continues the whimsical yet profound tradition.

Other thinkers concentrated on ruthless efficiency in government and came to be known as Legalists. One major Legalist thinker was Han Feizi. His book, the *Han Feizi*, condemns ideas from other schools of thought that had devolved into practices that were considered wasteful, corrupt, and inefficient. In response, he speaks directly to the highest levels of leadership, using Daoist terminology and fable-like stories to make his points, advising rulers on how to motivate people, how to organize the government and the military, and how to protect their own positions of power.

Still other thinkers concentrated their theories on military strategy and tactics. The major representative of this genre is, of course, Sunzi, and his classic *Art of War*, a text that so profoundly and succinctly examines how to get the greatest competitive advantage with the least harm done that it is still read today by military leaders and captains of industry.

The political, military, and intellectual battles continued throughout the Warring States Period in a complex interplay until Han Feizi's version of Legalism seemed to tip the balance for the Qin. But the victory was short-lived, and soon a version of Confucianism would rise to the top as the preferred philosophy of political elites. But Daoism, and later Buddhism, had their own periods of dominance and influenced many aspects of Chinese culture over the centuries.

II. ZHUANGZI AND HIS IDEAS

Some texts in world literature stand out as so unique and influential that they are at once emblematic of a culture and universal in scope: Shakespeare's plays, the *Bhagavad Gita*, the Book of Job, Plato's Socratic dialogues, the *Dhammapada*. If you were asked to name such a book from the Chinese tradition, the *Zhuangzi* probably isn't the first book to spring to mind simply because it is not that well-known. Instead, you would probably think of the *Analects* of Confucius, Laozi's *Daodejing*, maybe the great Tang Dynasty poems, or *Dream of the Red Chamber*. All good choices, but the *Zhuangzi* is no less important or influential than those others. The text is named after its author, Zhuang Zhou—Zhuangzi, for short. It is like a cross between Aesop's *Fables* and Ludwig Wittgenstein's *Philosophical Investigations*. Some of the most profound and challenging ideas are laid out in the form of colorful characters and episodes and have been so influential in Chinese literature, art, and philosophy that they have entered the language in the form of sayings that roll off the tongue of farmers and PhDs alike.

We know very little about the man Zhuang Zhou except that he lived during the 4th century BCE and was engaged with the intellectual scene of his time. That scene revolved around questions of good government. Like their Greek contemporaries, educated Chinese had a chance to influence the government in significant ways. Greeks lived in a *polis* (an independent city-state) and acted politically through a stumbling democracy. Chinese lived in a *guo* 國 (an enfeoffed state) and acted politically through a stumbling meritocracy under a hereditary monarch. Confucians and Mo-ists (followers of Mozi) dominated discussions about good government—discussions which branched out into the nature of language, the basic make-up of human beings, and how to build a moral and competent leader. Many Confucians thought they had a lock on the moral side of things, advocating a government underpinned by ritual propriety (*li* 禮). Many Mo-ists thought they had a lock on the linguistic side of things, dominating discussions through arch logical arguments. Zhuangzi came along and dropped a grenade on both schools of thought, questioning the universality of moral and linguistic categories and cautioning his contemporaries about unintended consequences stemming from overconfidence in one's way of conceiving the world and managing it through those conceptions.

Confucians traditionally held elaborate funeral ceremonies as an expression of respect for and devotion to the deceased. Mo-ists railed against the unnecessary expense. Zhuangzi's response? We see on the very last page (233) of this book Zhuangzi telling his friends to simply lay him out on the ground after he dies. Radical. Outrageous. But what is the difference between Zhuangzi's suggestion and our process today? Buried bodies—even embalmed ones—get consumed by other organisms. Zhuangzi shows us that our customs and conventions, while comfortable and even useful, tend to be arbitrary. It is, therefore, misguided to rely on them as the one and only guide for action. And so, a theme we see in the *Zhuangzi* is the flouting of convention: Zhuangzi drums after his wife dies (p. 129), a great painter strips off his clothes before working (p. 163), capable people reject offers of powerful jobs in the government (p. 122). The specific reasons for the flouting of convention in each of these episodes are different, but the general reason is the same: not all conventions are as useful, benign, or advantageous as they are often made out to be. Sometimes they can be inflexible, wrongheaded, and even personally harmful.

Conventions and customs (including the very words we use to label the world (p. 15)) can lock us into inflexible ways of thinking, and the creativity we see in Zhuangzi is the ability to see beyond them. Zhuangzi finds new uses for "useless" things (p. 19) and sees old problems from new perspectives. Can virtues be harmful instead of helpful (p. 87)? Can a valuable pearl be dangerous instead of beneficial (p. 230)? Can something be accomplished through non-action (*wu wei* 無為) instead of action (p. 103)?

What does Zhuangzi mean by "non-action"? Customs and conventions can be grouped under the umbrella category: *artificial*. To "non-" something for Zhuangzi is to undo the artificial, to return to a more natural way of doing things. Non-action, non-governing, non-thinking, non-interference—these all mean to strip away the clever, intentional, one-size-fits-all solution and to do only what the situation calls for. The cook carving up the cow (p. 41) is the classic example of non-action. We see it also in the old wheelwright (p. 96), the cicada-catcher (p. 140), and the bell-stand maker (p. 146). Each one empties himself of desire and expectation—anything that could interfere with the operation itself—and responds only to the requirements of the moment. Zhuangzi says we should use the mind like a mirror (p. 77)—reflecting only what is in front of us and not bringing along any extraneous thoughts, worries, hopes, or fears. This is how we return to the natural.

The obvious objection you may have of equating the natural with the good probably involves the many examples of things that are natural but not good: poisons, mosquitoes, aging, earthquakes, cancer, shark attacks, etc. This is where we can see how Zhuangzi differs from so many other religions/philosophies. According to Christianity, humans are born sinful. In Islam, humans must submit themselves to the wishes of Allah. In Hinduism and much of Buddhism, the world we live in is an illusory world of suffering. By contrast, we see in Zhuangzi (and in Chinese philosophy broadly), the belief that the world is pretty darn good just as it is. Why? Because everything more or less fits together so that all things (more or less) can flourish for a time. Then they decline and other things flourish. Everything is in a particular phase of a particular cycle. Everything is always changing. It is only because of these cycles and changes that any one thing—including you and I—can ever flourish at all.

So, from a narrow point of view, focused on any particular thing that happens to be on the down side of a cycle—growing old, getting cancer, being attacked by a shark—nature can seem dangerous and unforgiving. But my aging and dying makes room for the next human being. The random mutations that result in cancer can also result in evolutionary adaptation. My being eaten by a shark feeds that shark. From the larger perspective, the cycles continue, which is a good thing—because they make all good things (as viewed from narrow perspectives) possible.

This is not a variety of pre-determined fate. There is no author, no designer, no grand plan (pp. 98, 191). There is no "reason" that I get eaten by a shark. No "reason" that I get cancer. Zhuangzi is fine with the idea that stuff just happens. That's the nature of nature. But just as nature is not determined, nature is also not entirely random. To Zhuangzi, nature (*tian* 天) is a self-organizing spontaneity (*ziran* 自然). It has a rhythm and a generativity, and we can tap into it. The word Zhuangzi (and other early Chinese) used for this generative rhythm is *dao* 道. Many times in this book, we see Zhuangzi and others refer to "the Dao." This is what they mean—a rhythm of the universe,

a kind of roughly predictable logic, a way that things work, a path that each individual thing takes through its existence. The universe has the Dao, which is, more or less, good because it is the ground for all of the good things we have in life. A government or a person can be more or less in tune with the Dao; and being more in tune with it increases the chances of its people flourishing. How to be in tune with the Dao? Non-action, non-interference, non-striving, and so on. Reduce your desires and expectations. Find your own specific path and pursue that. Are you a cicada-catcher? Then catch cicadas. Are you a wheel-maker? Then make wheels. Empty yourself of all social expectations and personal desires and just be yourself. Move according to your natural mechanism (p. 114). Each particular thing has its particular Dao (pp. 33, 134). If each thing follows it, then all things will naturally flourish (more or less, at least for a time). Humans have the dubious distinction of being able to fall off their path by trying too hard, by pursuing limitless desires, by wanting too much. Scale it back, Zhuangzi says. Don't bring yourself grief (unless your path entails that for a time (p. 49)).

Getting good at non-doing can resemble a kind of spiritual practice. Zhuangzi even uses the term "spirit" (*shen* 神). *Shen* fundamentally refers to a kind of animating energy that can range in meaning from the energy that it takes to work hard (p. 103) to the vaguely supernatural (p. 122) to very definite spirits and gods. For Zhuangzi, to reduce desires, to follow your specific path, to be yourself, is to nurture your spirit rather than exhausting it. A well-nurtured spirit can come through particular practices, as in Yan Hui's account of mental fasting (p. 48) and his "sitting in forgetting" (p. 73), or it can simply be there naturally (pp. 62, 103, 139). Either way, you are getting at what is already there.

Why, by the way, is Yan Hui—Confucius's prized disciple—depicted as a follower of Zhuangzi's philosophy? Even Confucius humbles himself to Laozi. What's going on? The easy answer is that Zhuangzi is just borrowing these characters and putting them to his own use. The more complicated—and interesting—answer is that there is some overlap between the philosophy of Zhuangzi and Confucius. But wasn't Confucius a

Confucian and Zhuangzi a Daoist, and aren't those two philosophies in direct opposition to one another? Actually, no.

Confucius wasn't a Confucian because really there is no such thing as "Confucianism," per se. He is known as a *ru* 儒, a term that we translate into English as "Confucian" but which does not refer to the person of Confucius. Properly speaking, we should say that Confucius's beliefs belong to Ruism, not Confucianism. Also, Zhuangzi did not identify as a Daoist; in fact, there was no such school of thought during his time. That label came along later and was applied to him retrospectively. Both Zhuangzi and Confucius (and most other early Chinese thinkers) encouraged people to follow the Dao. In that sense, they were both little-d daoists. But what we now call Daoism has an emphasis on the very broad perspective of natural cycles and individual paths, whereas what we call Confucianism focuses more on the intermediate realm of ordering human society (but still, when done well, in harmony with natural cycles and individual human paths). The difference between the two schools of thought was more a difference in emphasis than a difference in dogma. In fact, over Chinese history, intellectuals tended to emphasize one or the other depending on their stage of life or their opportunities in a more just or less just society. If the "Dao was in the world," then they would feel safe working in government and taking on a Confucian perspective. If the "Dao was not in the world," they would retreat to the safety of a reclusive, Daoist lifestyle. Unlike so many other religions and philosophies around the world that see each other as mutually exclusive and even fight wars over their disagreements, Daoists and Confucians tend to see themselves as two sides of the same coin. But Daoists, as we see in *Zhuangzi* (pp. 62, 208), are not averse to calling out the narrowness and inflexibility that tends to crop up when Confucians over-emphasize custom and convention.

III. THE ARTIST AND HIS WORK

When I was a kid and the daily newspaper was dropped at our doorstep, I loved reading the comic strips and the political cartoons. They could be cute, amusing, and insightful all at once. When I came across C. C. Tsai's illustrated versions of the Chinese classics, I recognized the same brilliant combination of wit and wisdom and fell in love with his books.

I would be remiss if I finished this introduction without introducing the inimitable Chih-chung Tsai (蔡志忠), who goes by "C. C." in English, and whose own story is as amazing as anything he depicts in his books. The way he tells it, he knew at the age of five that he would draw for a living, and, at the age of fifteen, his father gave him permission to drop out of school and move from their small town to the metropolis of Taipei, where a comic publisher had welcomed him after receiving an unsolicited manuscript, not realizing how young he was. The young C. C. developed his own humorous comic book characters, all the while honing his skills and learning from other illustrators. During a required three-year stint in the military, he devoted his free time to educating himself in art history and graphic design. On leaving the military he tested into a major movie and television production company, beating out other applicants with their formal educations. There, he had the good fortune of coming across a cache of Disney films, and taught himself animation. Soon he was making his own short films, and then decided to open his own animation studio, winning Taiwan's equivalent of the Oscar just two years later.

Always looking for a new challenge, C. C. began a syndicated comic strip, which quickly expanded to five different strips in magazines and newspapers across Southeast Asia. At the height of his popularity as a syndicated cartoonist, he turned in yet another direction—the illustration of the Chinese classics in comic book format. They were an instant success and propelled him to the top of the bestseller list. That's what you have in your hand.

According to C. C., the secret to his success is not ambition, or even hard work. It's just about having fun and following his interests. One of his interests has been studying the classics. Remember, he dropped out of middle school. By ordinary standards, he should be unable to grasp the language of ancient China. The early Chinese wrote in a language that is to contemporary Chinese as Latin is to contemporary Spanish or Italian.

But he is a tireless autodidact, with a nearly photographic memory. He knows as much about the Chinese classics as many PhDs in the field. The main difference between him and a tenured professor is that he isn't interested in the refined disputes and distinctions on which scholars spend their careers. He merely wants to understand the ideas and share them with others. This book, and others in the series, is the result of playtime in his modest studio—serious and lighthearted, whimsical and profound all at once.

In working with the classics, C. C. stays close to tradition, and in his illustrations he more or less follows the prominent commentaries. This means that the texts that underpin his books are pretty much the same as the texts that underpin other translations you will find on bookstore shelves, with incidental differences here and there that are insignificant to the overall meaning.

C. C. translated the Classical language into contemporary Chinese so that the average reader could understand it. While respecting his interpretive choices where there is ambiguity, I've also chosen to translate with an eye to the Classical language, rather than just from his contemporary Chinese. This helps avoid the attenuation of meaning that happens when communication goes through too many steps—like in the "telephone" game that children play.

In the *Zhuangzi*, stories are used to illustrate particular points and are embedded in larger contexts. C. C. pulls the story out, illustrates it in a series of panels, and then sums up the moral of the story in the final balloon. For the summary, C. C. draws from the original context and traditional commentaries to make the idea relevant to a contemporary reader. The reader should have full confidence that each episode comes straight out of the *Zhuangzi* with little alteration. As with his other adaptations, the advantage that C. C.'s versions of the classics have over regular, text-only editions is the visual dimension that brings the reader directly into the world of the ancients.

I hope that you enjoy this English version of C. C.'s illustrated *Zhuangzi* as much as so many others have enjoyed the original Chinese version.

THE WAY OF
NATURE

ZHUANGZI

莊子者，蒙人也，名周。周嘗為蒙漆園吏，與梁惠王、齊宣王同時。其學無所不闚，然其要本歸於老子之言。故其著書十餘萬言，大抵率寓言也。作漁父、盜跖、胠篋，以詆訿孔子之徒，以明老子之術。畏累虛、亢桑子之屬，皆空語無事實。然善屬書離辭，指事類情，用剽剝儒、墨，雖當世宿學不能自解免也。其言洸洋自恣以適己，故自王公大人不能器之。

【史記·老子韓非列傳】

THE NAME OF OUR HERO IS ZHUANG ZHOU. LIKE ALL CHINESE NAMES THE SURNAME COMES FIRST, FOLLOWED BY THE GIVEN NAME. TO SHOW RESPECT FOR HIS VAST WISDOM, WE ADD THE WORD "ZI" TO HIS SURNAME, JUST LIKE KONGZI (CONFUCIUS), MENGZI (MENCIUS), AND LAOZI. ZHUANGZI LIVED DURING THE FOURTH CENTURY BCE, A TIME KNOWN AS THE WARRING STATES PERIOD IN CHINA. THIS WAS A PERIOD OF DISUNITY IN WHICH RIVAL NATIONS BATTLED CONSTANTLY FOR MORE LAND AND GREATER POWER. AS A RESULT, IT WAS ALSO A TIME OF WIDESPREAD DEATH AND DESTRUCTION. ZHUANGZI SAW THIS AND WAS DEEPLY SADDENED BY IT.

HE SHIFTED HIS LINE OF SIGHT FROM HUMAN SOCIETY TO THE LIMITLESSNESS OF TIME AND SPACE.

夫莊子者，可謂知本矣，故未始藏其狂言，言雖無會而獨應者也。夫應而非會，則雖當無用；言非物事，則雖高不行；與夫寂然不動，不得已而後起者，固有間矣，斯可謂知無心者也。夫心無為，則隨感而應，應隨其時，言唯謹爾。故與化為體，流萬代而冥物，豈曾設對獨遘而游談乎方外哉！此其所以不經而為百家之冠也。

郭象《莊子序》

4

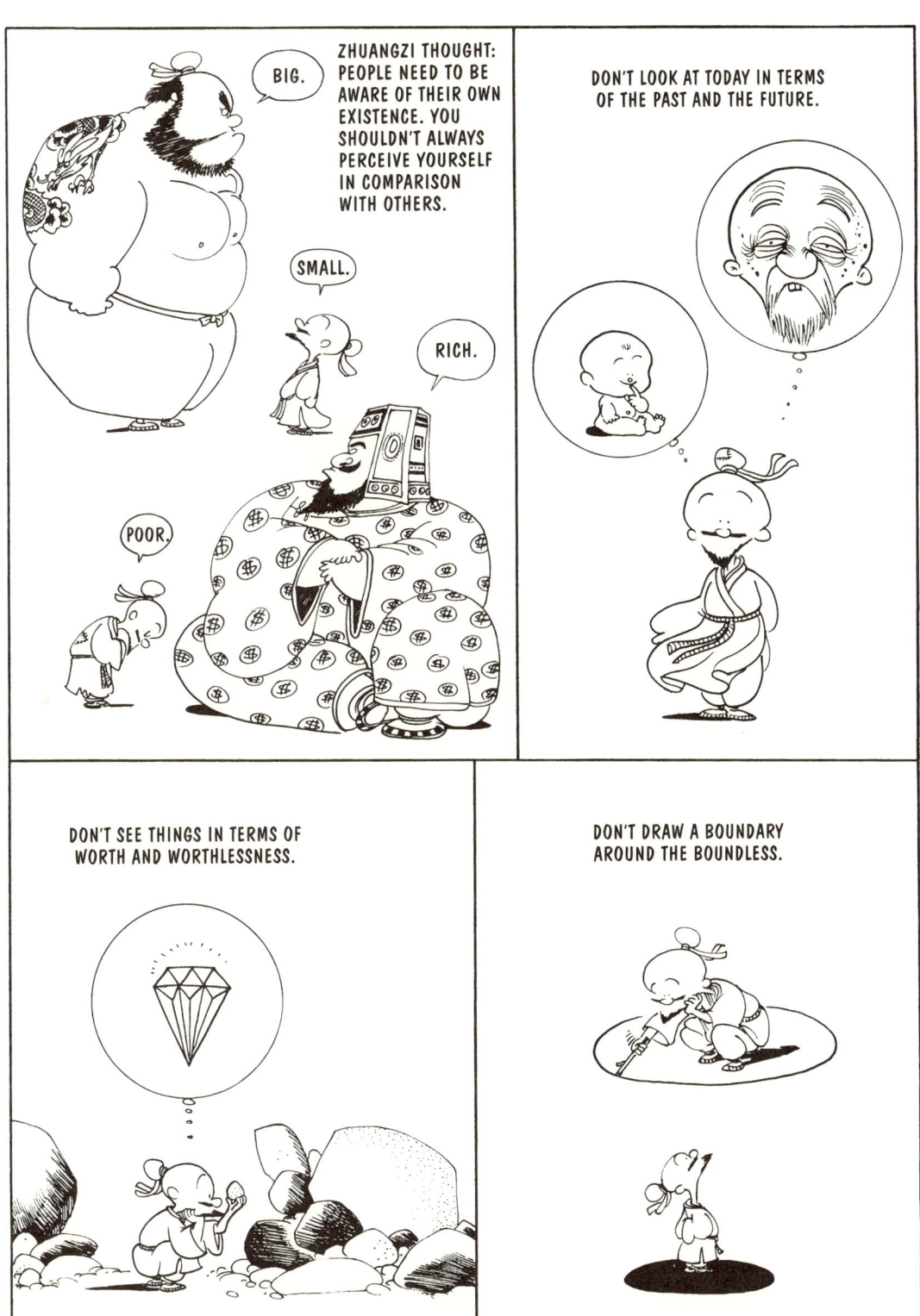

莊子者，姓莊，名周，（太史公云：字子休。）梁國蒙縣人也。六國時，為漆園吏，與魏惠王、齊宣王、楚威王同時，（李頤云：與齊愍王同時。）齊楚嘗聘以為相，不應。時人皆尚遊說，莊生獨高尚其事，優遊自得，依老氏之旨，著書十餘萬言，以逍遙自然無為齊物而已；大抵皆寓言，歸之於理，不可案文責也。

陸德明《莊子序》

DON'T DRAW LIFE FROM DEATH. ONLY IN THIS WAY CAN YOU ATTAIN LIMITLESS FREEDOM.

THE PHILOSOPHY OF ZHUANGZI IS A PHILOSOPHY OF FREEDOM. IT IS A PHILOSOPHY THAT TAKES LIFE AND HURLS IT INTO THE LIMITLESSNESS OF TIME AND SPACE IN ORDER TO BE EXPERIENCED TO THE FULLEST.

TO ZHUANGZI, HUMAN SOCIETY IS CHAINED BY A "LIFELESS ORDER," BUT WHAT HE PURSUED WAS A "LIVELY DISORDER."

CHAPTER 1

Carefree Living

北冥有魚，其名為鯤。鯤之大，不知其幾千里也。化而為鳥，其名為鵬。鵬之背，不知其幾千里也，怒而飛，其翼若垂天之雲。是鳥也，海運則將徙於南冥……。天之蒼蒼，其正色邪？其遠而無所至極邪？其視下也，亦若是則已矣。

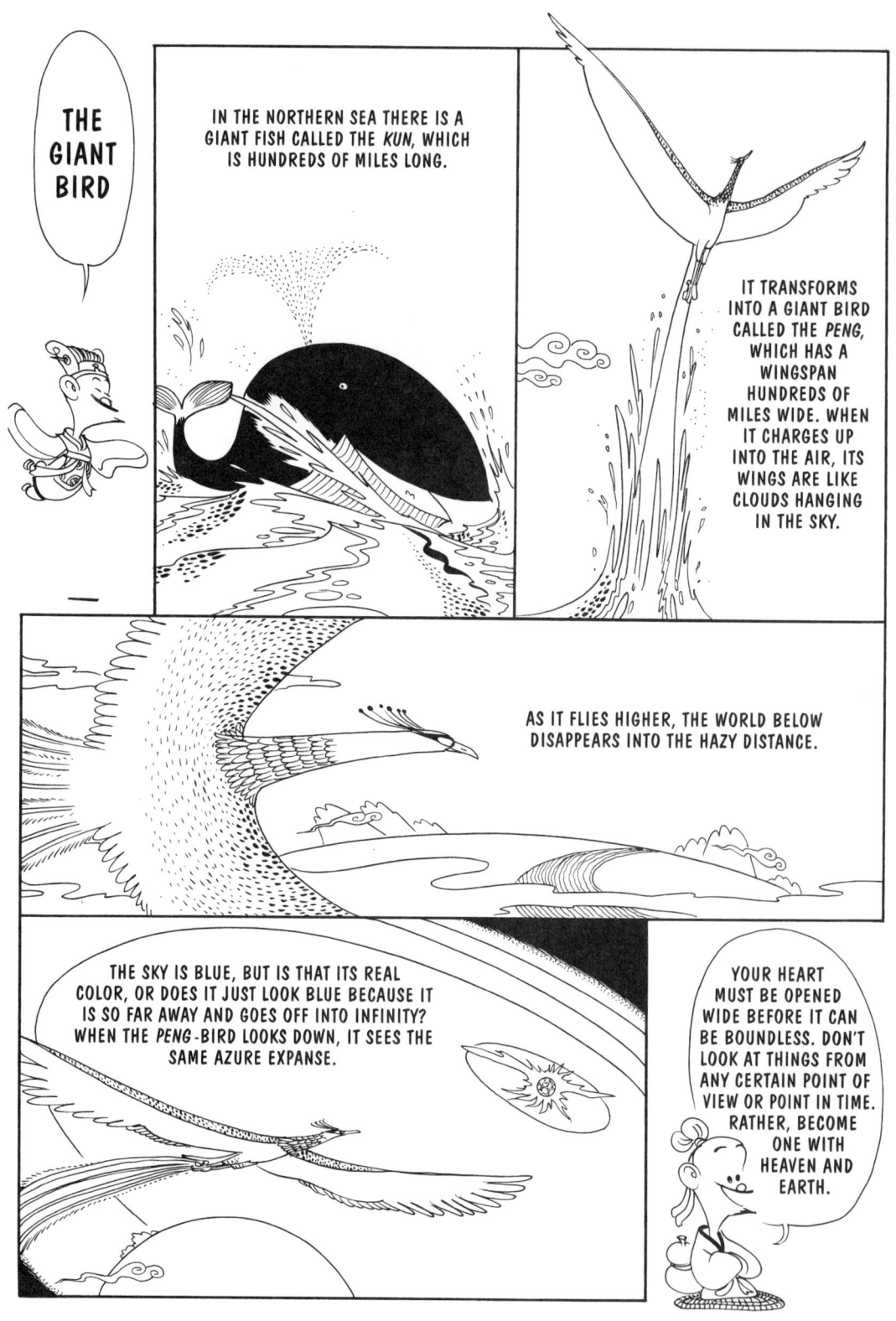

THE GIANT BIRD

IN THE NORTHERN SEA THERE IS A GIANT FISH CALLED THE *KUN*, WHICH IS HUNDREDS OF MILES LONG.

IT TRANSFORMS INTO A GIANT BIRD CALLED THE *PENG*, WHICH HAS A WINGSPAN HUNDREDS OF MILES WIDE. WHEN IT CHARGES UP INTO THE AIR, ITS WINGS ARE LIKE CLOUDS HANGING IN THE SKY.

AS IT FLIES HIGHER, THE WORLD BELOW DISAPPEARS INTO THE HAZY DISTANCE.

THE SKY IS BLUE, BUT IS THAT ITS REAL COLOR, OR DOES IT JUST LOOK BLUE BECAUSE IT IS SO FAR AWAY AND GOES OFF INTO INFINITY? WHEN THE *PENG*-BIRD LOOKS DOWN, IT SEES THE SAME AZURE EXPANSE.

YOUR HEART MUST BE OPENED WIDE BEFORE IT CAN BE BOUNDLESS. DON'T LOOK AT THINGS FROM ANY CERTAIN POINT OF VIEW OR POINT IN TIME. RATHER, BECOME ONE WITH HEAVEN AND EARTH.

小知不及大知，小年不及大年。
以五百歲為春，五百歲為秋；
奚以知其然也？朝菌不知晦朔，
蟪蛄不知春秋，此小年也。楚之南有冥靈者，

9

上古有大椿者，以八千歲為春，八千歲為秋。而彭祖乃今以久特聞，眾人匹之，不亦悲乎！

有鳥焉，其名為鵬，背若泰山，翼若垂天之雲，摶扶搖羊角而上者九萬里，絕雲氣，負青天，然後圖南，且適南冥也。斥鴳笑之曰：「彼且奚適也？我騰躍而上，不過數仞而下，翱翔蓬蒿之間，此亦飛之至也。而彼且奚適也？」此小大之辯也。

11

若夫乘天地之正，而御六氣之辯，以遊無窮者，彼且惡乎待哉！故曰：至人無己，神人無功，聖人無名。

夫列子御風而行，泠然善也，旬有五日而後反。彼於致福者，未數數然也。此雖免乎行，猶有所待者也。

LIEZI RIDES THE WIND

LIEZI COULD FLY BY SIMPLY CATCHING A BREEZE, AND WHAT A BEAUTIFUL SIGHT IT WAS.

HE COULD FLY AWAY AND NOT RETURN FOR FIFTEEN DAYS. SUCH JOY IS VERY RARE.

BUT TO A PERSON OF THE DAO, LIEZI STILL WASN'T COMPLETELY FREE.

ALTHOUGH HE DIDN'T HAVE TO USE HIS LEGS TO WALK, HE STILL HAD TO DEPEND ON THE WIND TO FLY.

LIEZI COULD FLY, BUT NOT WITHOUT THE WIND. IF WE ACT IN ACCORDANCE WITH THE NATURAL DAO, WE WILL UNDERSTAND THE PRINCIPLES OF EVERYTHING, WHICH WILL ALLOW US TO TRAVEL IN A BOUNDLESS REALM WITHOUT DEPENDING ON ANYTHING.

堯讓天下於許由，曰：「日月出矣，而爝火不息，其於光也，不亦難乎！時雨降矣，而猶浸灌，其於澤也，不亦勞乎！夫子立而天下治，而我猶尸之，吾自視缺然。請致天下。」

許由曰：「子治天下，天下既已治也。而我猶代子，吾將為名乎？名者，實之賓也。吾將為賓乎？鷦鷯巢於深林，不過一枝；偃鼠飲河，不過滿腹。歸休乎君，予無所用天下為！庖人雖不治庖，尸祝不越樽俎而代之矣。」

13

宋人資章甫而適諸越，越人斷髮文身，無所用之。堯治天下之民，平海內之政，往見四子藐姑射之山，汾水之陽，窅然喪其天下焉。

THE TATTOOED YUE PEOPLE

ONE DAY, A MAN FROM SONG WENT TO THE SOUTHERN STATE OF YUE TO SELL HATS AND SHIRTS, THINKING HE COULD MAKE LOTS OF MONEY.

GET YER SHIRTS! BEEYOOTEEFUL AND FASHIONABLE HATS AND SHIRTS FOR SALE!

WHAT HE DIDN'T KNOW WAS THAT THE YUE PEOPLE HAD A CUSTOM OF CUTTING THEIR HAIR SHORT

AND NOT WEARING SHIRTS BECAUSE THEY TATTOOED THEIR BODIES.

USELESS JUNK.

USEFUL AND USELESS, ACHIEVEMENT AND FAILURE, ARE ALL RELATIVE, AND NONE ARE NECESSARILY CONSISTENT OVER TIME. THE ACHIEVEMENT AND FAILURE OF THE LEGENDARY KINGS YAO AND SHUN ARE LIKE THE USEFULNESS AND USELESSNESS OF THE SONG MAN'S GARMENTS. NOTHING IS FOR SURE.

USEFUL USELESS

HUIZI'S GIANT GOURDS

HUIZI WAS AN OLD FRIEND OF ZHUANGZI.

ONE DAY, THE KING GAVE ME SOME SEEDS OF THE GIANT CALABASH.

I PLANTED THEM, AND THE CALABASHES TURNED OUT TO BE HUGE. ONE OF THEM ALONE COULD HOLD FIVE GALLONS.

BUT THEY WERE WEAK, AND IF YOU FILLED THEM WITH WATER, THEY'D BREAK AS SOON AS YOU PICKED THEM UP.

AND THEY COULDN'T BE CUT IN HALF TO BE USED AS LADLES BECAUSE THEY WERE TOO BRITTLE.

THE CALABASHES MAY HAVE BEEN BIG BUT THEY WERE TOO BIG, SO BIG THAT THEY WERE USELESS. SO I THREW THEM AWAY.

惠子謂莊子曰：「魏王貽我大瓠之種，我樹之成而實五石，以盛水漿，其堅不能自舉也。剖之以為瓢，則瓠落無所容。非不呺然大也，吾為其無用而掊之。」

莊子曰：「夫子固拙於用大矣……。

今子有五石之瓠，何不慮以為大樽而浮乎江湖，而憂其瓠落無所容？

則夫子猶有蓬之心也夫！」

16

THE SONG FAMILY'S SECRET FORMULA

IN THE STATE OF SONG, THERE LIVED A FAMILY WHO KNEW HOW TO MAKE A CERTAIN KIND OF MEDICINE.

THIS MEDICINE COULD PROTECT THE SKIN FROM CRACKING AND CHAFING FROM PROLONGED EXPOSURE TO COLD WATER.

KEEPING THIS MEDICINE TO THEMSELVES, GENERATION AFTER GENERATION OF THE SONG FAMILY DID A BUSINESS IN CLOTH BLEACHING.

THEN ONE DAY, A TRAVELER FOUND OUT ABOUT THE FORMULA FOR THE MEDICINE AND BOUGHT IT FOR ONE HUNDRED GOLD PIECES.

THIS IS WORTH A FORTUNE!

HE PRESENTED THE SECRET FORMULA TO THE KING OF WU AND EXPLAINED HOW IT COULD BE USED IN A MILITARY CAMPAIGN.

宋人有善為不龜手之藥者，世世以洴澼絖為事。客聞之，請買其方百金。聚族而謀曰：『我世世為洴澼絖，不過數金；今一朝而鬻技百金，請與之。』客得之，以說吳王。

17

越有難，吳王使之將，冬與越人水戰，大敗越人，裂地而封之。能不龜手，一也；或以封，或不免於洴澼絖，則所用之異也。

AT THAT TIME, THE STATES OF WU AND YUE WERE BITTER ENEMIES.

AFTER GETTING THE SECRET FORMULA FOR THIS MEDICINE, THE KING OF WU LAUNCHED A WINTER OFFENSIVE BY WATER.

THE WU ARMY RELIED ON THIS MEDICINE TO PREVENT FROSTBITE, BUT THE YUE SOLDIERS WERE UNPROTECTED. AS A RESULT, THE YUE ARMY WAS ROUNDLY DEFEATED.

AFTER THE DEFEAT OF THE YUE KINGDOM, THE TRAVELER WHO PRESENTED THE SECRET FORMULA TO THE KING OF WU WAS REWARDED WITH A LARGE ESTATE, AND LIVED THE LIFE OF A NOBLEMAN THEREAFTER.

ALTHOUGH IT WAS THE SAME FORMULA, SOME PEOPLE DIDN'T KNOW HOW TO USE IT, SO THEY SPENT THEIR LIVES BLEACHING CLOTH. BUT WHEN A FLEXIBLE PERSON WHO COULD THINK OF NEW IDEAS CAME ALONG, HE ENDED UP LIVING THE LIFE OF A WEALTHY MAN.

惠子謂莊子曰：「吾有大樹，人謂之樗。

其大本擁腫而不中繩墨，其小枝卷曲而不中規矩，立之塗，匠者不顧。

今子之言，大而無用，眾所同去也。」

THE USELESS *SHU* TREE

HUIZI ONCE SAID TO ZHUANGZI:

I HAVE THIS GIANT TREE CALLED A *SHU* TREE. ITS TRUNK IS ALL LUMPS AND BUMPS AND IT WINDS THIS WAY AND THAT.

ITS BRANCHES ARE ALL GNARLED AND TWISTED. A CARPENTER'S PLUMB LINE COULD NEVER BE USED ON IT.

IT GROWS RIGHT BESIDE THE ROAD, AND NO CARPENTER HAS EVER PAID ANY ATTENTION TO IT.

THE WORDS YOU HAVE BEEN SPEAKING LATELY ARE JUST LIKE THIS TREE, BIG AND USELESS. WHO'S GOING TO LISTEN TO YOU?

莊子曰：「子獨不見狸狌乎？卑身而伏，以候敖者；東西跳梁，不避高下，中於機辟，死於罔罟。今夫斄牛，其大若垂天之雲。此能為大矣，而不能執鼠。

HUIZI, HAVE YOU EVER SEEN A FOX OR A WILDCAT?

IN ORDER TO CATCH THEIR PREY, THEY ARE ALWAYS JUMPING OVER THINGS AND RUNNING ALL OVER THE PLACE. ALTHOUGH THEY ARE VERY AGILE...

EVENTUALLY, THEY WILL FALL INTO A TRAP AND DIE.

AS FOR THE YAK, ALTHOUGH IT IS BIG, LIKE A GIANT CLOUD HANGING IN THE SKY,

IT COULDN'T CATCH A MOUSE IF IT WANTED TO.

今子有大樹，患其無用，何不樹之於無何有之鄉，廣莫之野，彷徨乎無為其側，逍遙乎寢臥其下。不夭斤斧，物無害者，無所可用，安所困苦哉！」

YOU HAVE THIS GREAT BIG TREE, AND YOU'RE WORRIED THAT IT'S USELESS. WHY NOT REST UNDER IT AND USE IT FOR SHELTER AND SHADE?

SINCE THE TREE IS "USELESS," NO ONE WILL COME ALONG AND CHOP IT DOWN, SO NATURALLY, THERE'S NOTHING TO WORRY ABOUT.

...

THERE'S NOTHING THE *SHU* TREE COULD BE USED FOR, SO IT WASN'T CHOPPED DOWN. TO THE *SHU* TREE, USING USELESSNESS WAS ITS GREATEST ADVANTAGE.

CHAPTER 2

On Seeing Things Evenly

南郭子綦隱几而坐，仰天而噓，嗒焉似喪其耦。顏成子游立侍乎前，曰：「何居乎？形固可使如槁木，而心固可使如死灰乎？今之隱几者，非昔之隱几者也。」子綦曰：「偃，不亦善乎，而問之也！今者吾喪我，汝知之乎？女聞人籟而未聞地籟，女聞地籟而未聞天籟夫！」

23

子游曰：「敢問其方。」子綦曰：「夫大塊噫氣，其名為風。是唯無作，作則萬竅怒呺。而獨不聞之翏翏乎？山林之畏佳，大木百圍之竅穴，似鼻，似口，似耳，似枅，似圈，似臼，似洼者，似污者，

24

激者，謞者，叱者，吸者，叫者，譹者，宎者，咬者，前者唱于而隨者唱喁。泠風則小和，飄風則大和，厲風濟則眾竅為虛。而獨不見之調調，之刁刁乎？」

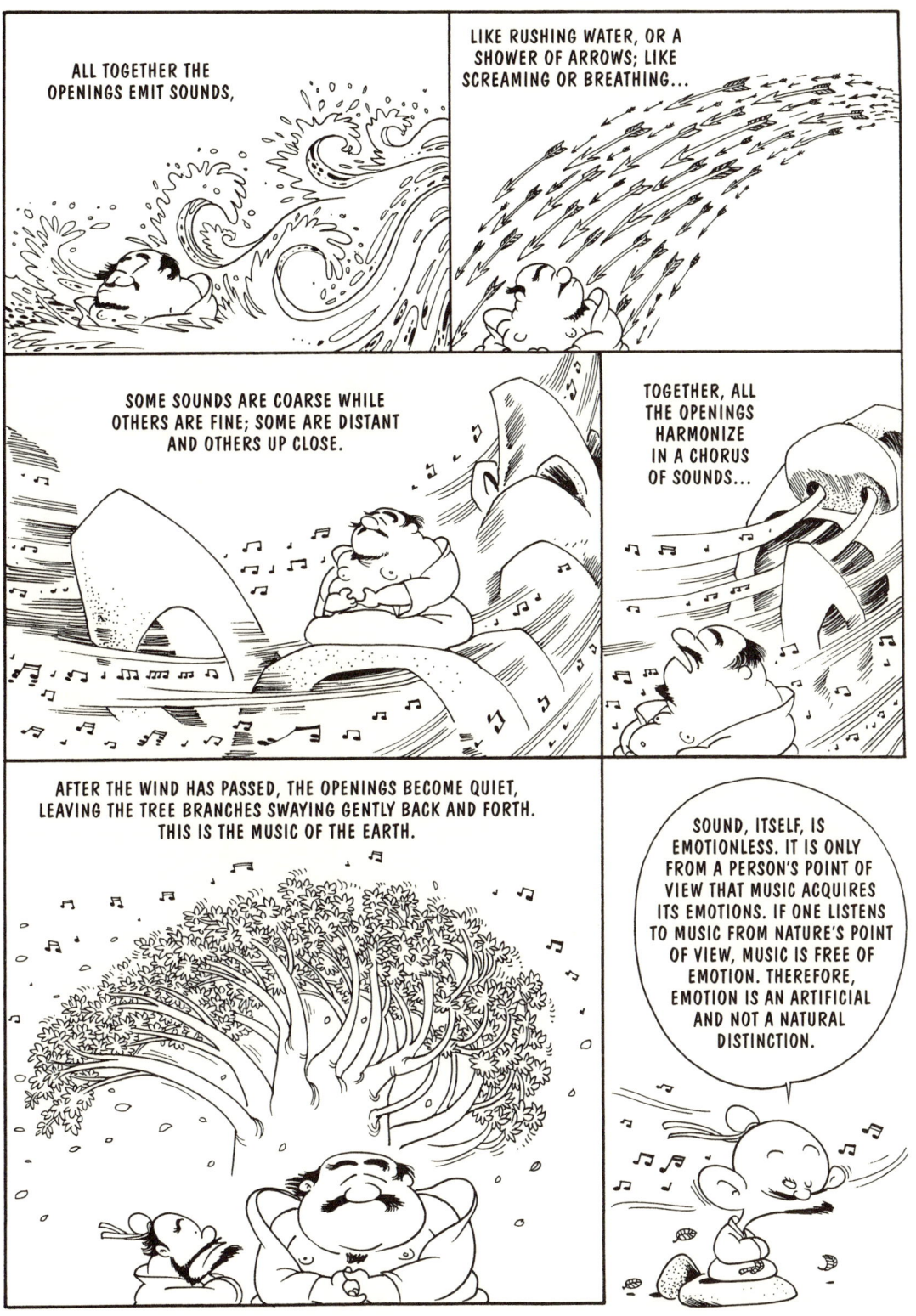

百骸，九竅，六藏，賅而存焉，吾誰與為親？汝皆說之乎？其有私焉？如是皆有為臣妾乎？其臣妾不足以相治乎？其遞相為君臣乎？其有真君存焉？如求得其情與不得，無益損乎其真。

WHO'S THE MASTER?

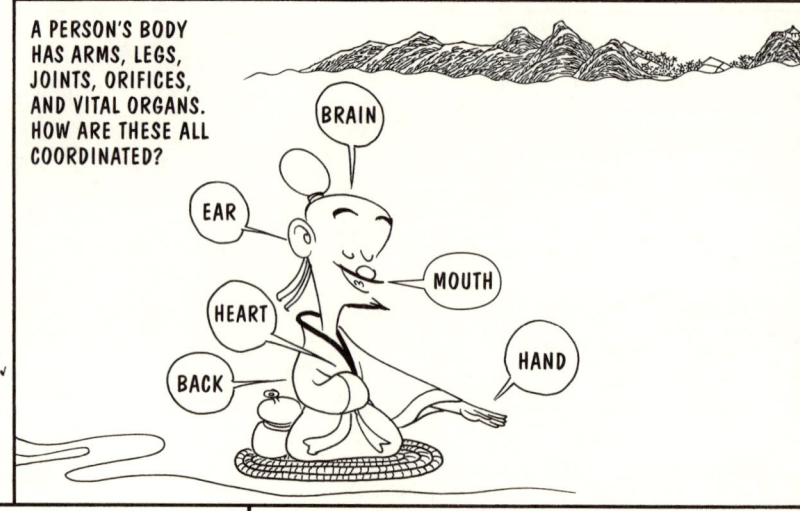

A PERSON'S BODY HAS ARMS, LEGS, JOINTS, ORIFICES, AND VITAL ORGANS. HOW ARE THESE ALL COORDINATED?

BRAIN

EAR

MOUTH

HEART

HAND

BACK

ARE THEY ALL THERE TO SERVE ME? HOW CAN SERVANTS BE COORDINATED?

DO THEY TAKE TURNS COORDINATING EACH OTHER? OR IS THERE A GENUINE MASTER THAT CONTROLS THEM ALL?

WHETHER OR NOT WE COME TO KNOW THIS MASTER WILL NOT ALTER ITS GENUINENESS ONE WAY OR THE OTHER.

EVERYONE HAS THEIR OWN GENUINE MIND, WHICH IS A MINIATURE OF THE NATURAL DAO. SO, IF YOU CAN ACT IN ACCORDANCE WITH IT, YOU WILL NEVER BE FAR FROM THE DAO.

IS XI SHI REALLY BEAUTIFUL?

IF FROM THE BEGINNING WE HAD CALLED THE SKY "HORSE"

HORSE

HORSE

AND CALLED THE GROUND "FINGER"

FINGER

FINGER

THEN THE SKY WOULD BE "HORSE" AND THE GROUND WOULD BE "FINGER."

HORSE

FINGER

WHEN PEOPLE THINK THAT SOMETHING IS WRONG, THEY SAY "WRONG." AND WHEN THEY THINK THAT SOMETHING IS RIGHT, THEY SAY "RIGHT." BUT WHAT ARE THE STANDARDS OF "RIGHT" AND "WRONG"?

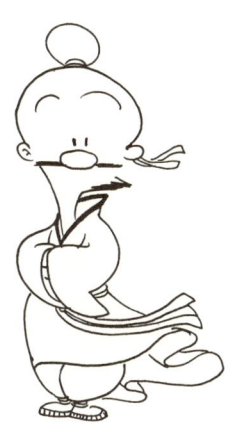

PEOPLE THINK THAT XI SHI IS BEAUTIFUL, BUT WHAT WOULD A FISH THINK? IF A FISH SAW XI SHI, IT MIGHT VERY WELL SWIM AWAY IN DISGUST.

GORGEOUS!

GROSS!

IN CREATING KNOWLEDGE FROM A HUMAN STANDPOINT, PEOPLE TRAP THEMSELVES IN THEIR OWN LIMITED WORLD.

天地，一指也；萬物，一馬也。可乎可，不可乎不可。道行之而成，物謂之而然。惡乎然？然於然。惡乎不然？不然於不然。物固有所然，物固有所可。無物不然，無物不可。故為是舉莛與楹，厲與西施，恢恑憰怪，道通為一。！

27

唯達者知通為一，為是不用而寓諸庸。庸也者，用也；用也者，通也；通也者，得也；適得而幾矣。因是已。已而不知其然，謂之道。勞神明為一而不知其同也，謂之朝三。何謂朝三？曰狙公賦芧，曰：「朝三而莫四。」眾狙皆怒。曰：「然則朝四而莫三。」眾狙皆悅。名實未虧而喜怒為用，亦因是也。是以聖人和之以是非而休乎天鈞，是之謂兩行。

古之人，其知有所至矣。惡乎至？有以為未始有物者，至矣，盡矣，不可以加矣。其次以為有物矣，而未始有封也。其次以為有封焉，而未始有是非也。是非之彰也，道之所以虧也。道之所以虧，愛之所以成。果且有成與虧乎哉？果且無成與虧乎哉？有成與虧，故昭氏之鼓琴也；無成與虧，故昭氏之不鼓琴也。

29

昭文之鼓琴也，師曠之枝策也，惠子之據梧也，三子之知幾乎，皆其盛者也。

今且有言於此，不知其與是類乎？其與是不類乎？類與不類，相與為類，則與彼無以異矣。雖然，請嘗言之。有始也者，有未始有始也者，有未始有夫未始有始也者。有有也者，有無也者，有未始有無也者，有未始有夫未始有無也者。俄而有無矣，而未知有無之果孰有孰無也。今我則已有謂矣，而未知吾所謂之其果有謂乎，其果無謂乎？天下莫大於秋豪之末，而大山為小；莫壽乎殤子，而彭祖為夭。天地與我並生，而萬物與我為一。既已為一矣，且得有言乎？既已謂之一矣，且得無言乎？一與言為二，二與一為三。自此以往，巧歷不能得，而況其凡乎！故自無適有以至於三，而況自有適有乎！無適焉，因是已。

31

故昔者堯問於舜曰：「我欲伐宗、膾、胥敖，南面而不釋然。其故何也？」舜曰：「夫三子者，猶存乎蓬艾之間。若不釋然，何哉？昔者十日並出，萬物皆照，而況德之進乎日者乎！」

YAO'S QUESTION

THE LEGENDARY EMPEROR YAO ONCE ASKED HIS MINISTER SHUN:

I WANT TO INVADE THE THREE STATES OF ZONG, KUAI, AND XU'AO, AND EVERY TIME I SIT ON THE THRONE, I CAN'T GET IT OUT OF MY HEAD. WHY IS THIS?

THE SOVEREIGNS OF THOSE THREE STATES ARE SMALL FRY COMPARED TO YOU. WHY EVEN BOTHER WITH THEM?

THAT PEOPLE HAVE INFINITE DESIRES STEMS ENTIRELY FROM A SENSE OF "SELF." AS SOON AS THERE IS A "SELF," ONE TENDS TO REJECT "OTHERS." ALL THINGS IN NATURE ARE UNIQUE, AND EACH HAS ITS OWN PARTICULAR VALUE. THIS IS WHY WE CAN ALL SHINE WITHOUT BLOCKING EACH OTHER OUT.

ORIGINALLY, WHEN THERE WERE TEN SUNS SHINING DOWN ON THE MYRIAD THINGS, THEY NEVER BLOCKED EACH OTHER OUT. SO HOW IS IT THAT A VIRTUOUS MAN, WHOSE MAGNANIMITY SHINES DOWN ON ALL PEOPLE EVEN IN PLACES THE SUN DOESN'T REACH, CANNOT TOLERATE THREE OTHER STATE SOVEREIGNS?

齧缺問乎王倪曰：「子知物之所同是乎？」曰：「吾惡乎知之！」「子知子之所不知邪？」曰：「吾惡乎知之！」「然則物無知邪？」曰：「吾惡乎知之！雖然，嘗試言之。庸詎知吾所謂知之非不知邪？庸詎知吾所謂不知之非知邪？且吾嘗試問乎女：民溼寢則腰疾偏死，鰌然乎哉？木處則惴慄恂懼，猨猴然乎哉？

33

三者孰知正處？民食芻豢，麋鹿食薦，蝍且甘帶，鴟鴉耆鼠，四者孰知正味？猨猵狙以為雌，麋與鹿交，鰌與魚游。毛嬙、麗姬，人之所美也；魚見之深入，鳥見之高飛，麋鹿見之決驟。四者孰知天下之正色哉？自我觀之，仁義之端，是非之塗，樊然殽亂，吾惡能知其辯！

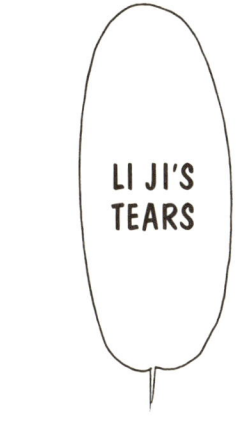

LI JI'S TEARS

I'M NOT MARRYING HIM! I WON'T DO IT!

ON LI JI'S WEDDING DAY, SHE WAS TO BE MARRIED AGAINST HER WILL TO DUKE XIAN OF JIN. SHE WAS SO SAD THAT SHE DRENCHED HER WEDDING DRESS IN TEARS.

BUT AFTER SHE WAS MARRIED, SHE FOUND HERSELF SLEEPING ON A BIG, SOFT BED AND EATING FOOD FROM THE FOUR CORNERS OF THE EARTH. WHO WOULD BELIEVE THAT ON HER WEDDING DAY, SHE HAD CRIED HER EYES OUT?

EVERYONE IS AFRAID OF DYING, BUT MAYBE DEATH WILL BE SO GREAT THAT WE'LL END UP REGRETTING HAVING EVER LIVED.

予嘗為女妄言之，女以妄聽之，奚？旁日月，挾宇宙，為其脗合，置其滑涽，以隸相尊。眾人役役，聖人愚芚，參萬歲而一成純。萬物盡然，而以是相蘊。予惡乎知說生之非惑邪！予惡乎知惡死之非弱喪而不知歸者邪！麗之姬，艾封人之子也。晉國之始得之也，涕泣沾襟；及其至於王所，與王同筐床，食芻豢，而後悔其泣也。予惡乎知夫死者不悔其始之蘄生乎！

35

夢飲酒者，旦而哭泣；夢哭泣者，旦而田獵。方其夢也，不知其夢也。夢之中又占其夢焉，覺而後知其夢也。且有大覺而後知此其大夢也，而愚者自以為覺，竊竊然知之。君乎，牧乎，固哉！丘也與女，皆夢也；予謂女夢，亦夢也。是其言也，其名為弔詭。萬世之後而一遇大聖，知其解者，是旦暮遇之也。

ZHANG WUZI'S DREAM

ZHANG WUZI SAID TO JU QUE:

A PERSON HAVING A DREAM IS NEVER AWARE OF IT, AND IN HIS DREAM HE MIGHT EVEN DO THINGS LIKE PREDICT HIS OWN FATE. ONLY AFTER HE WAKES UP DOES HE REALIZE THAT HE WAS DREAMING.

ONLY THE TRULY ENLIGHTENED PERSON REALIZES THAT LIFE IS JUST ONE BIG DREAM. AND THEN THERE ARE THOSE FOOLS WHO THINK THAT THEY ARE THE ENLIGHTENED ONES.

YOU'RE DREAMING!

YOU AND I ARE BOTH DREAMING. WHEN I SAY YOU ARE DREAMING, THAT IS MERE DREAM TALK.

ONLY THOSE WHO HAVE GREAT DOUBTS CAN TRULY BE ENLIGHTENED. BUT A FOOL ALWAYS BELIEVES THAT HE IS ENLIGHTENED, AND THAT IS WHY, IN THE END, HE IS A FOOL.

SHADOWS TALKING

WANG LIANG IS THE SHADOW OF A SHADOW.

HEY, HEY, HEY!

WOULD YOU MAKE UP YOUR MIND WHAT YOU WANT TO DO?! FIRST YOU WALK, THEN YOU STOP, THEN YOU SIT, THEN YOU STAND. I CAN'T TAKE IT!

LOOK, I CAN'T HELP IT. I'M JUST FOLLOWING HIM.

A SNAKE DEPENDS ON ITS SCALES TO SLITHER, A CICADA DEPENDS ON ITS WINGS TO FLY.

BUT AFTER THEY DIE, EVEN THOUGH THE SCALES AND WINGS STILL REMAIN, THEY CAN NEITHER SLITHER NOR FLY.

CHANGE IS A LAW OF NATURE. THERE IS NO DESIGNATED KING OR MINISTER. WHAT IS NATURAL IS DECIDING WHETHER YOU ARE A LEADER OR A FOLLOWER.

罔兩問景曰：「曩子行，今子止；曩子坐，今子起，何其無特操與？」景曰：「吾有待而然者邪？吾所待又有待而然者邪？吾待蛇蚹蜩翼邪？惡識所以然！惡識所以不然！」

37

昔者莊周夢為胡蝶，栩栩然胡蝶也，自喻適志與！不知周也。俄然覺，則蘧蘧然周也。不知周之夢為胡蝶與，胡蝶之夢為周與？周與胡蝶，則必有分矣。此之謂物化。

THE DREAM OF THE BUTTERFLY

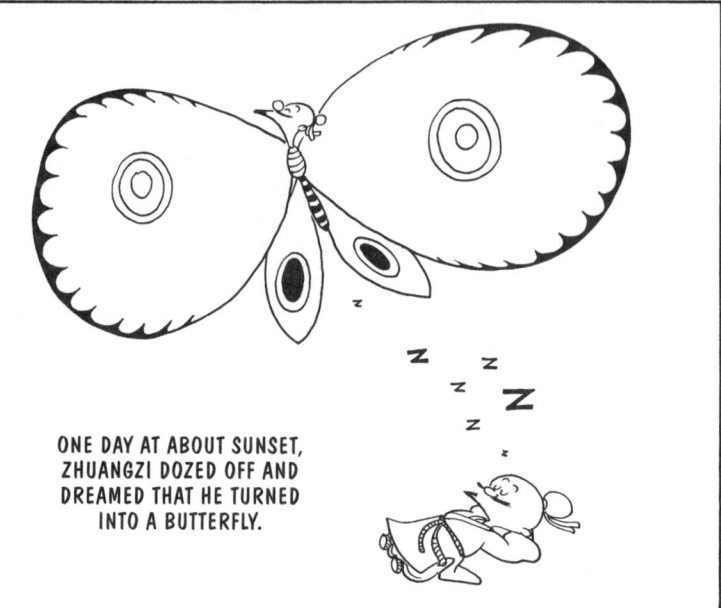

ONE DAY AT ABOUT SUNSET, ZHUANGZI DOZED OFF AND DREAMED THAT HE TURNED INTO A BUTTERFLY.

HE FLAPPED HIS WINGS, AND SURE ENOUGH, HE WAS A BUTTERFLY—WHAT A JOYFUL FEELING! AS HE FLUTTERED ABOUT, HE COMPLETELY FORGOT THAT HE WAS ZHUANGZI.

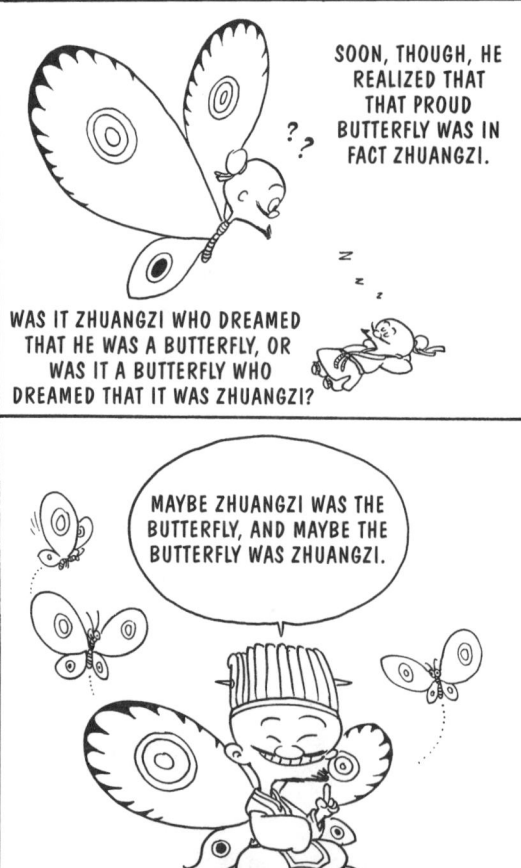

SOON, THOUGH, HE REALIZED THAT THAT PROUD BUTTERFLY WAS IN FACT ZHUANGZI.

WAS IT ZHUANGZI WHO DREAMED THAT HE WAS A BUTTERFLY, OR WAS IT A BUTTERFLY WHO DREAMED THAT IT WAS ZHUANGZI?

MAYBE ZHUANGZI WAS THE BUTTERFLY, AND MAYBE THE BUTTERFLY WAS ZHUANGZI.

CHAPTER 3

The Basics of
Nurturing Life

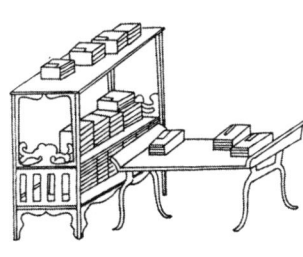

吾生也有涯，而知也無涯。以有涯隨無涯，殆已；已而為知者，殆而已矣。為善無近名，為惡無近刑。緣督以為經，可以保身，可以全生，可以養親，可以盡年。

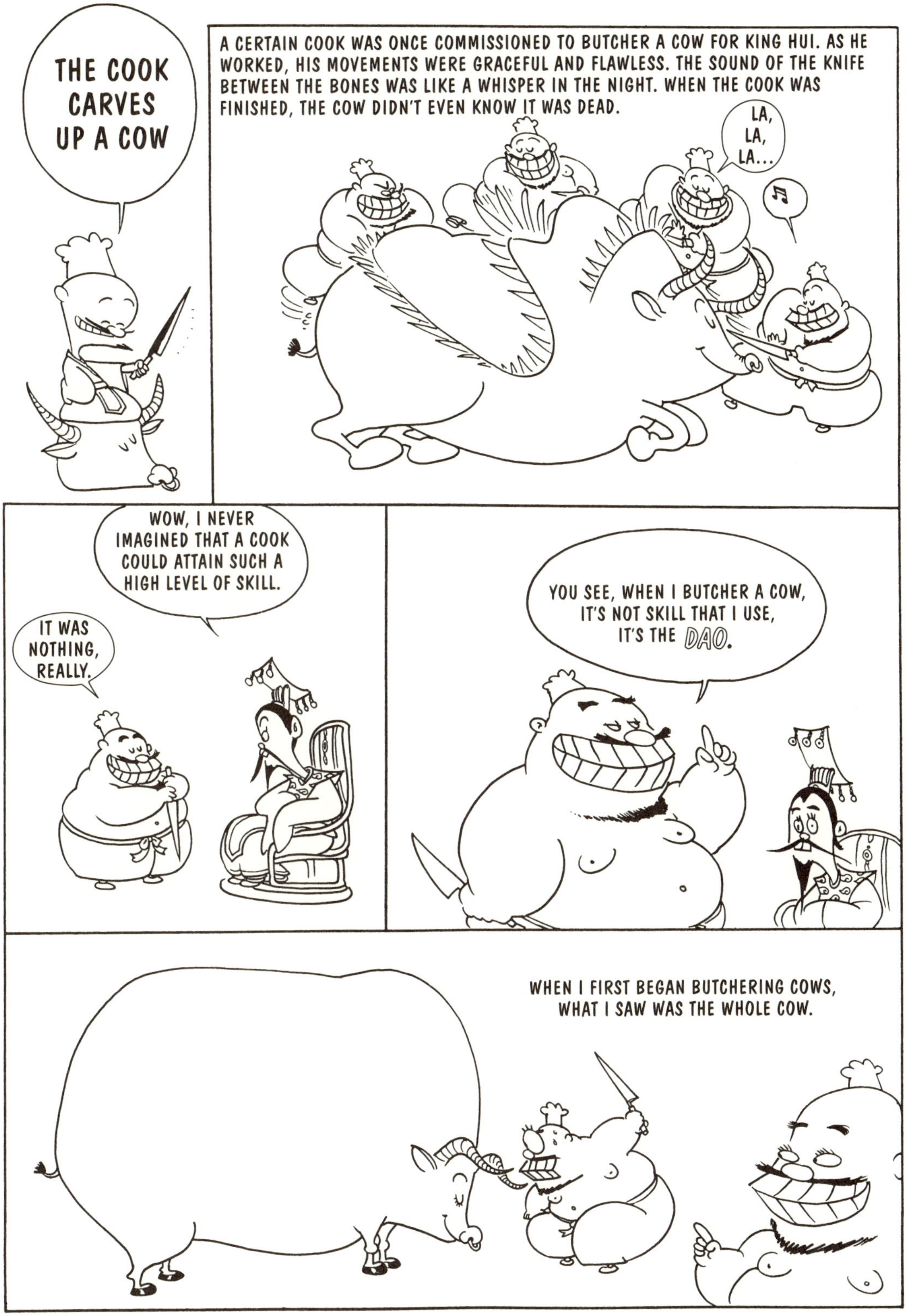
THE COOK CARVES UP A COW
A CERTAIN COOK WAS ONCE COMMISSIONED TO BUTCHER A COW FOR KING HUI. AS HE WORKED, HIS MOVEMENTS WERE GRACEFUL AND FLAWLESS. THE SOUND OF THE KNIFE BETWEEN THE BONES WAS LIKE A WHISPER IN THE NIGHT. WHEN THE COOK WAS FINISHED, THE COW DIDN'T EVEN KNOW IT WAS DEAD.
LA, LA, LA...
♪
WOW, I NEVER IMAGINED THAT A COOK COULD ATTAIN SUCH A HIGH LEVEL OF SKILL.
IT WAS NOTHING, REALLY.
YOU SEE, WHEN I BUTCHER A COW, IT'S NOT SKILL THAT I USE, IT'S THE DAO.
WHEN I FIRST BEGAN BUTCHERING COWS, WHAT I SAW WAS THE WHOLE COW.

CHAPTER 3
THE BASICS OF
NURTURING LIFE

庖丁為文惠君解牛，手之所觸，肩之所倚，足之所履，膝之所踦，砉然嚮然，奏刀騞然，莫不中音。合於桑林之舞，乃中經首之會。文惠君曰：「譆，善哉！技蓋至此乎？」庖丁釋刀對曰：「臣之所好者道也，進乎技矣。始臣之解牛之時，所見非牛者。三年之後，未嘗見全牛也。方今之時，臣以神遇而不以目視，官知止而神欲行。依乎天理，批大郤，導大窾，因其固然。技經肯綮之未嘗，而況大軱乎！

良庖歲更刀，割也：：族庖月更刀，折也。今臣之刀十九年矣，所解數千牛矣，而刀刃若新發於硎。彼節者有間，而刀刃者無厚；以無厚入有間，恢恢乎其於遊刃必有餘地矣，是以十九年而刀刃若新發於硎。雖然，每至於族，吾見其難為，怵然為戒，視為止，行為遲。動刀甚微，謋然已解，如土委地。提刀而立，為之四顧，為之躊躇滿志，善刀而藏之。」文惠君曰：「善哉！吾聞庖丁之言，得養生焉。」

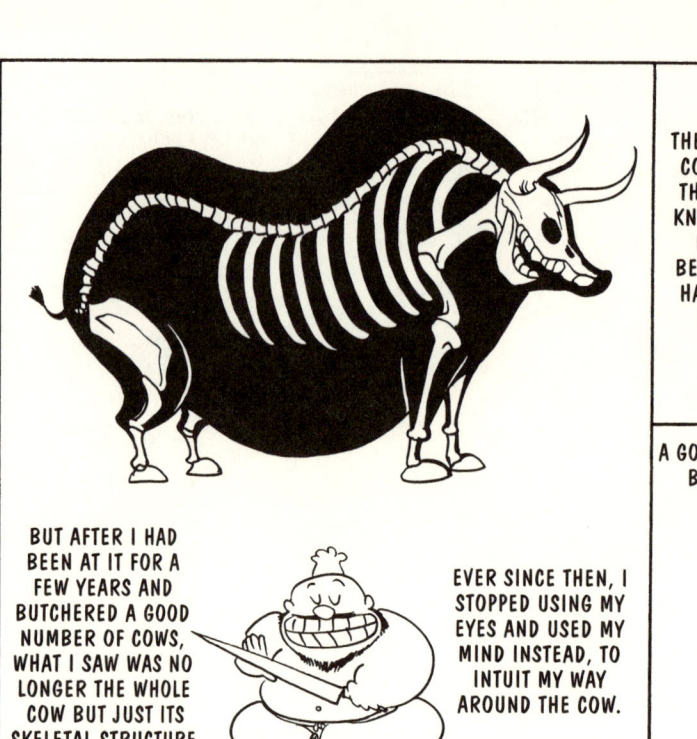

THE AVERAGE COOK GOES THROUGH A KNIFE EVERY MONTH, BECAUSE HE HACKS AND CHOPS.

A GOOD COOK CHANGES KNIVES ONCE A YEAR, BECAUSE HE CHOPS BUT DOESN'T HACK.

BUT AFTER I HAD BEEN AT IT FOR A FEW YEARS AND BUTCHERED A GOOD NUMBER OF COWS, WHAT I SAW WAS NO LONGER THE WHOLE COW BUT JUST ITS SKELETAL STRUCTURE.

EVER SINCE THEN, I STOPPED USING MY EYES AND USED MY MIND INSTEAD, TO INTUIT MY WAY AROUND THE COW.

BECAUSE I NEITHER HACK NOR CHOP, I'VE USED THIS SAME KNIFE FOR NINETEEN YEARS, AND IT'S STILL LIKE NEW.

BARELY ONE MONTH ...

NINETEEN YEARS.

MY KNIFE GLIDES IN AND OUT BETWEEN THE BONE JOINTS, MOVING AS IT PLEASES; THE COW SUFFERS NO PAIN AND, IN THE END, DOESN'T EVEN KNOW IT'S DEAD.

FANTASTIC! WHAT YOU HAVE SAID TODAY HAS TAUGHT ME A LOT ABOUT HOW TO GET ALONG IN LIFE.

THE COMPLEXITIES OF LIFE ARE LIKE THE SKELETAL STRUCTURE OF THE COW, AND THOSE WHO DON'T UNDERSTAND HOW TO APPROACH THEM END UP RUNNING AROUND IN CIRCLES, WASTING ALL THEIR ENERGY.

THE MAN WITH ONE LEG

WHEN GONGWEN XUAN FIRST SAW AN OFFICIAL WITH ONLY ONE LEG, HE WAS VERY SURPRISED...

THEN AFTER THINKING ABOUT IT, HE FINALLY REALIZED...

HE MAY ONLY HAVE ONE LEG, BUT AS LONG AS HE WAS BORN THAT WAY RATHER THAN HAVING HAD IT CUT OFF AS PUNISHMENT FOR A CRIME, IT IS IN ACCORDANCE WITH NATURE!

IF EVERYONE WERE BORN WITH ONE LEG, WE WOULD THINK IT VERY UNNATURAL TO SUDDENLY SEE SOMEONE WITH TWO LEGS. AS LONG AS SOMEONE IS BORN THE WAY THEY ARE, BE IT WITH ONE LEG, TWO LEGS, OR AS MANY LEGS AS A MILLIPEDE, IT IS NATURAL.

WE HAVE TO LIVE WITH THE BODY WE WERE BORN WITH AND DEAL WITH CIRCUMSTANCES AS THEY COME. IF WE CAN DO THIS, THEN WE WON'T FEEL COLD IN WATER OR HOT IN FIRE, AND WE WILL ENCOUNTER NO OBSTACLES IN LIFE.

CHAPTER 3
THE BASICS OF NURTURING LIFE

公文軒見右師而驚曰：「是何人也？惡乎介也？天與，其人與？」曰：「天也，非人也。天之生是使獨也，人之貌有與也。以是知其天也，非人也。」

43

澤雉十步一啄，百步一飲，不蘄畜乎樊中。神雖王，不善也。

老聃死，秦失弔之，三號而出。弟子曰：「非夫子之友邪？」曰：「然。」「然則弔焉若此，可乎？」曰：「然。始也吾以為其人也，而今非也。向吾入而弔焉，有老者哭之，如哭其子；少者哭之，如哭其母。彼其所以會之，必有不蘄言而言，不蘄哭而哭者。是遁天倍情，忘其所受，古者謂之遁天之刑。適來，夫子時也；適去，夫子順也。安時而處順，哀樂不能入也，古者謂是帝之縣解。」

45

指窮於為薪，火傳也，不知其盡也。

PASSING ON THE FLAME

WHEN OIL IS USED TO SUSTAIN A FLAME,

EVEN THOUGH THE OIL MAY BE CONSUMED,

THE FLAME CAN BE TRANSFERRED TO ANOTHER FUEL.

WHO KNOWS HOW LONG IT CAN GO ON?

DAO!

DAO!

DAO!

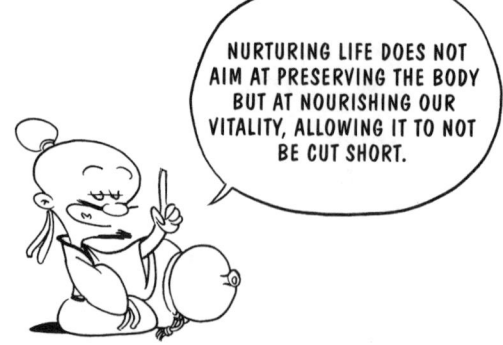

NURTURING LIFE DOES NOT AIM AT PRESERVING THE BODY BUT AT NOURISHING OUR VITALITY, ALLOWING IT TO NOT BE CUT SHORT.

CHAPTER 4
In Human Society

聽止於耳，心止於符。
氣也者，虛而待物者也。
唯道集虛。虛者，心齋也。」
非心齋也。」回曰：「敢問心齋？」仲尼曰：「若一志，無聽之以耳而聽之以心，無聽之以心而聽之以氣！
暞天不宜。」顏回曰：「回之家貧，唯不飲酒不茹葷者數月矣。若此，則可以為齋乎？」曰：「是祭祀之齋，
輕用其國，而不見其過。」
顏回見仲尼，請行。曰：「奚之？」曰：「將之衛。」曰：「奚為焉？」曰：「回聞衛君，其年壯，其行獨，
吾無以進矣，敢問其方。」仲尼曰：「齋，吾將語若！有而為之，其易邪？易之者，

MENTAL FASTING

BECAUSE THE SOVEREIGN OF WEI WAS VERY WICKED, YAN HUI ASKED CONFUCIUS...

MASTER, PLEASE LET ME GO REFORM HIM!

OF COURSE YOU CAN GO, BUT I'M AFRAID THAT IF YOU GO WITH THE INTENTION OF REFORMING HIM, IT WILL BE DIFFICULT.

WHY DON'T YOU GO HOME AND FAST FOR A FEW DAYS, AND THEN WE'LL TALK ABOUT IT?

BUT BECAUSE I COME FROM A POOR FAMILY, IT HAS ALREADY BEEN SEVERAL MONTHS SINCE I'VE HAD ANY ALCOHOL OR MEAT.

THAT IS THE FASTING TO BE DONE FOR SACRIFICIAL CEREMONIES. IT'S NOT MENTAL FASTING.

WHAT IS MENTAL FASTING?

FIRST, GET RID OF ALL INTENTIONAL MENTAL ACTIVITY AND MAKE YOUR MIND AN EXPANSE OF EMPTINESS, THEN YOU WILL BE ABLE TO RESPOND NATURALLY TO EVERYTHING. IF YOU CAN DO THIS, THEN OTHERS WILL RESPOND TO YOU.

ACTING INTENTIONALLY MEANS ACTING WITH THE SELF IN MIND, WHICH WILL CAUSE YOU TO BE CONSCIOUS OF GAIN AND LOSS. WE SHOULD ELIMINATE THE EGO AND NOT WORK FOR ACHIEVEMENT, FAME, OR THE SELF. IF WE CAN DO THIS, THEN WE CAN TRANSFORM OTHERS.

葉公子高將使於齊，問於仲尼曰：「王使諸梁也甚重⋯⋯。今吾朝受命而夕飲冰，我其內熱與！吾未至乎事之情，而既有陰陽之患矣。事若不成，必有人道之患。是兩也，為人臣者不足以任之，子其有以語我來！」仲尼曰：「天下有大戒二。其一，命也；其一，義也。子之愛親，命也，不可解於心；臣之事君，義也，無適而非君也，無所逃於天地之間。是之謂大戒。是以夫事其親者，不擇地而安之，孝之至也；夫事其君者，不擇事而安之，忠之盛也⋯⋯。為人臣子者，固有所不得已。行事之情而忘其身，何暇至於悅生而惡死！夫子其行可矣！

49

町畦；彼且為無崖，亦與之為無崖。

為崩為蹶。心和而出，且為聲為名，為妖為孽。彼且為嬰兒，亦與之為嬰兒；彼且為無

慎之，正女身哉！形莫若就，心莫若和。雖然，之二者有患。就不欲入，和不欲出。形就而入，且為顛為滅，

則危吾身。其知適足以知人之過，而不知其所以過。若然者，吾奈之何？」蘧伯玉曰：「善哉問乎！戒之，

顏闔將傅衛靈公大子，而問於蘧伯玉曰：「有人於此，其德天殺。與之為無方，則危吾國；與之為有方，

50

達之，入於無疵。汝不知夫螳螂乎？怒其臂以當車轍，不知其不勝任也，是其才之美者也。戒之，慎之！積伐而美者以犯之，幾矣。」

FIRST GET HIM TO THINK THAT YOU AND HE ARE CUT FROM THE SAME CLOTH, THEN YOU CAN SLOWLY WIN HIM OVER.

HA HA HA!

WHY DO I HAVE TO BE SO FRIENDLY AND COOPERATIVE AT THE BEGINNING?

HAVE YOU EVER SEEN A MANTIS? IF ANGERED, IT WILL OVERESTIMATE ITS STRENGTH AND FIGHT WITH ANYTHING, EVEN AN ONCOMING CART.

NOW, IF YOU OVERESTIMATE YOUR ABILITIES AND CONFRONT THIS PERSON HEAD ON, WOULDN'T THAT BE LIKE A MANTIS TRYING TO STOP A CART?

WHEN ADVISING PEOPLE, USE DISCRETION. IF YOU ARE TOO FIRM, YOU'LL JUST PUSH THE SITUATION TO A CRISIS.

IT CAN BE DANGEROUS TO USE YOUR OWN ADVANTAGES TO PRESSURE ANOTHER PERSON INTO DOING SOMETHING.

汝不知夫養虎者乎？不敢以生物與之，為其殺之之怒也；不敢以全物與之，為其決之之怒也；時其飢飽，達其怒心。虎之與人異類而媚養己者，順也；故其殺者，逆也。

THE TIGER TRAINER

TRAINING TIGERS IS A VERY DANGEROUS BUSINESS. A PERSON WHO UNDERSTANDS THE ART OF TIGER TRAINING WOULD NEVER FEED A LIVE ANIMAL TO A TIGER.

THIS IS BECAUSE, IN THE ACT OF KILLING, A TIGER BECOMES INCENSED,

AND ONCE ITS KILLING INSTINCTS ARE AROUSED, THERE'S NO TURNING BACK.

THEREFORE, THE TRAINER ALWAYS TAKES HIS ANIMAL'S NATURE INTO ACCOUNT,

AND THE FEARSOME TIGER GROWS UP AS TAME AS A PUSSYCAT.

MEOW.

THAT'S A GOOD KITTY...

A TIGER HAS ITS NATURE, TOO, AND IF IT IS ATTENDED TO WITH CARE, THE TIGER WILL BE FRIENDLY INSTEAD OF FEARSOME.

THE HORSE LOVER

THERE WAS ONCE A MAN WHO LOVED HIS HORSE VERY MUCH.

夫愛馬者，以筐盛矢，以蜄盛溺。適有蚊虻僕緣，而拊之不時，則缺銜毀首碎胸。意有所至而愛有所亡，可不慎邪！

ONE DAY, WHEN THE MAN WENT TO SLAP A HORSEFLY OFF HIS HORSE'S BACKSIDE

BZZZ

HE WAITED ON IT HAND AND FOOT.

HE USED A WICKER BASKET TO CATCH THE HORSE'S DROPPINGS,

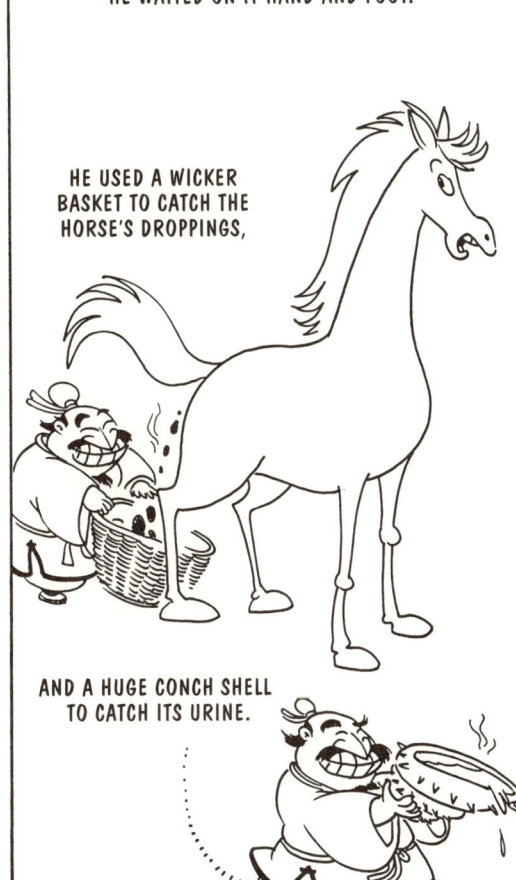

AND A HUGE CONCH SHELL TO CATCH ITS URINE.

THE HORSE WAS STARTLED

NEIGH!

AND KICKED THE MAN, WHO DIED INSTANTLY FROM THE BLOW.

YOU MAY LOVE A PERSON, BUT THAT PERSON WILL NOT NECESSARILY UNDERSTAND YOUR LOVE.

先生不肯視，行不輟，何邪？」曰：「已矣，勿言之矣！散木也。

觀者如市，匠伯不顧，遂行不輟。弟子厭觀之，走及匠石，曰：「自吾執斧斤以隨夫子，未嘗見材如此其美也。

匠石之齊，至乎曲轅，見櫟社樹。其大蔽數千牛，絜之百圍，其高臨山十仞而後有枝，其可以為舟者旁十數。

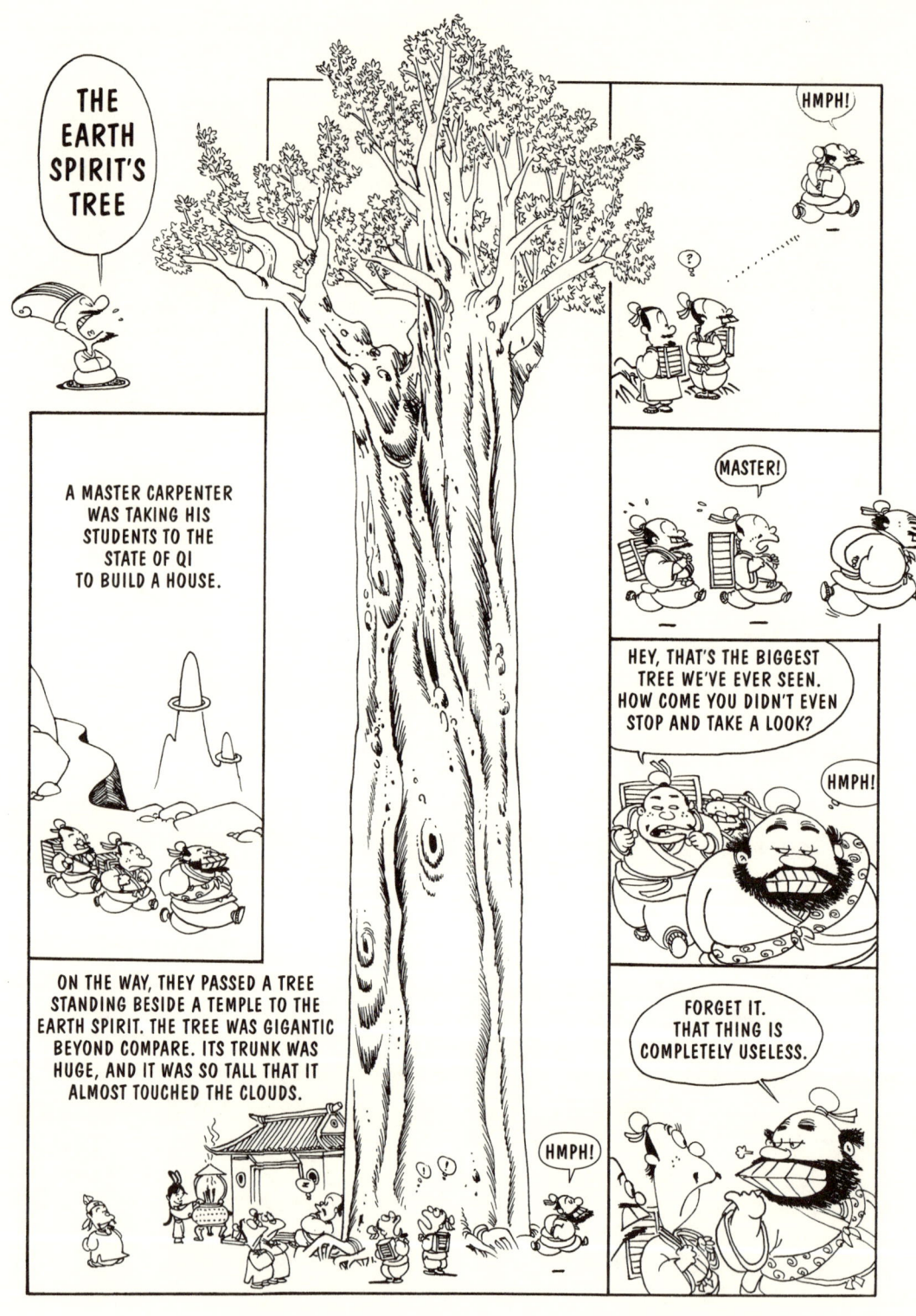

THE EARTH SPIRIT'S TREE

A MASTER CARPENTER WAS TAKING HIS STUDENTS TO THE STATE OF QI TO BUILD A HOUSE.

ON THE WAY, THEY PASSED A TREE STANDING BESIDE A TEMPLE TO THE EARTH SPIRIT. THE TREE WAS GIGANTIC BEYOND COMPARE. ITS TRUNK WAS HUGE, AND IT WAS SO TALL THAT IT ALMOST TOUCHED THE CLOUDS.

HMPH!

MASTER!

HEY, THAT'S THE BIGGEST TREE WE'VE EVER SEEN. HOW COME YOU DIDN'T EVEN STOP AND TAKE A LOOK?

HMPH!

FORGET IT. THAT THING IS COMPLETELY USELESS.

HMPH!

CHAPTER 4
IN HUMAN SOCIETY

以為舟則沈，以為棺槨則速腐，以為器則速毀，以為門戶則液樠，以為柱則蠹。是不材之木也，無所可用，故能若是之壽。」匠石歸，櫟社見夢曰：「女將惡乎比予哉？若將比予於文木邪？夫柤梨橘柚，果蓏之屬，實熟則剝，剝則辱，大枝折，小枝泄。此以其能苦其生者也，故不終其天年而中道夭，自掊擊於世俗者也。物莫不若是。且予求無所可用久矣，幾死，乃今得之，為予大用。使予也而有用，且得有此大也邪？且也若與予也皆物也，奈何哉其相物也？而幾死之散人，又惡知散木！」

貴人富商之家求禪傍者斬之。故未終其天年，而中道之夭於斧斤，此材之患也。

宋有荊氏者，宜楸柏桑。其拱把而上者，求狙猴之杙者斬之；三圍四圍，求高名之麗者斬之；七圍八圍，

A TREE'S NATURAL LIFE SPAN

IN SONG, THERE WAS A PLACE THAT WAS WELL SUITED FOR GROWING JAPONICA, CYPRESS, AND MULBERRY TREES. WHEN THESE TREES GREW TO A CERTAIN WIDTH, THEY WERE CUT DOWN AND USED TO BUILD MONKEY CAGES.

THE THICKER ONES WERE USED TO BUILD LARGE HOUSES.

IF THEY GREW EVEN THICKER, THEY WERE CUT DOWN AND USED TO MAKE COFFINS FOR THE RICH.

NONE OF THESE TREES EVER LIVED TO ENJOY A FULL NATURAL LIFESPAN, AND INSTEAD WERE CUT DOWN IN THE PRIME OF LIFE.

THOSE POOR USEFUL TREES ...

故解之以牛之白顙者與豚之亢鼻者，與人有痔病者不可以適河。此皆巫祝以知之矣，所以為不祥也。此乃神人之所以為大祥也。

IN ANCIENT TIMES, DURING THE SACRIFICE TO THE RIVER GOD, THE SHAMAN WOULD NEVER CHOOSE A COW WITH A WHITE FOREHEAD, A PIG WITH A LONG SNOUT, OR A PERSON WITH HEMORRHOIDS TO THROW INTO THE RIVER AS A SACRIFICE. THEY WERE CONSIDERED TO BE "INAUSPICIOUS."

INAUSPICIOUS CREATURES...

I HAVE A WHITE FOREHEAD.

I HAVE HEMORRHOIDS.

I HAVE A LONG SNOUT.

THE INTELLIGENT AND VERSATILE PERSON WOULD PRETEND TO BE UNFIT, OR INAUSPICIOUS, IN ORDER TO AVOID THIS SPIRITUAL DISASTER.

INAUSPICIOUS

INAUSPICIOUS

INAUSPICIOUS

BEAUTIFUL AND UGLY EACH HAVE THEIR OWN SPECIAL CHARACTERISTICS. IT'S NOT NECESSARY TO DISTINGUISH BETWEEN "GOOD" AND "BAD" AND "AUSPICIOUS" AND "INAUSPICIOUS."

IF A WOMAN IS CHOSEN TO BE SACRIFICED TO THE RIVER GOD BECAUSE OF HER BEAUTY, THEN IS BEAUTY AUSPICIOUS OR INAUSPICIOUS?

AUSPICIOUS?

INAUSPICIOUS?

支離疏者，頤隱於齊，肩高於頂，會撮指天，五管在上，兩髀為脅。挫鍼治繲，足以餬口；鼓筴播精，足以食十人。上徵武士，則支離攘臂於其間；上有大役，則支離以有常疾不受功；上與病者粟，則受三鍾與十束薪。夫支離其形者，猶足以養其身，終其天年，又況支離其德者乎！

THE FREAK

THERE ONCE WAS A VERY PECULIAR MAN NAMED ZHILI SHU, WHOSE BODY WAS TERRIBLY DEFORMED. HIS HEAD WAS BENT DOWN BELOW HIS NAVEL, HIS SHOULDERS REACHED UP ABOVE THE TOP OF HIS HEAD, HIS HAIR STUCK OUT IN ALL DIRECTIONS, HIS VITAL ORGANS WERE ALL OUT OF PLACE, AND HIS STOMACH HUNG DOWN BETWEEN HIS THIGHS.

BY HELPING PEOPLE WITH THEIR LAUNDRY, ZHILI SHU COULD MAKE ENOUGH MONEY TO GET BY.

AND BY TELLING FORTUNES, HE COULD SUPPORT A DOZEN PEOPLE.

VERY LUCKY, VERY LUCKY.

DURING TIMES OF WAR WHEN PEOPLE WERE CONSCRIPTED BY FORCE, ZHILI SHU SAUNTERED DOWN THE STREET KNOWING THAT NO ARMY WOULD WANT HIM.

HUMBY DEE DUM DUM.

DURING TIMES OF FAMINE WHEN THE GOVERNMENT GAVE OUT FREE GRAIN, ZHILI SHU WOULD BE FIRST IN LINE DUE TO HIS DISABILITY.

RICE

THE WISE PERSON DOESN'T CARE ABOUT AN UNAPPEALING ASPECT OR DISABILITY. THESE ATTRIBUTES CAN ALSO SAVE ONE FROM MUCH GRIEF AND HARDSHIP.

RIGHT!

孔子適楚，楚狂接輿遊其門曰：「鳳兮鳳兮，何如德之衰也！來世不可待，往世不可追也。天下有道，聖人成焉；天下無道，聖人生焉。方今之時，僅免刑焉。福輕乎羽，莫之知載；禍重乎地，莫之知避。已乎已乎，臨人以德！殆乎殆乎，畫地而趨！迷陽迷陽，無傷吾行！吾行郤曲，無傷吾足！」

59

山木自寇也，膏火自煎也。桂可食，故伐之；漆可用，故割之。人皆知有用之用，而莫知無用之用也。

OIL BURNS ITSELF OUT

A TREE BRANCH THAT IS MADE INTO AN AXE HANDLE ENDS UP CUTTING ITSELF DOWN.

OIL USED TO LIGHT A FIRE ENDS UP BURNING ITSELF AWAY.

THE CINNAMON TREE IS HEWN DOWN TO BE CONSUMED BY PEOPLE.

MMM, YUMMY!

THE VARNISH TREE THAT CAN PROTECT AGAINST DECAY ENDS UP SLASHED BY PEOPLE'S KNIVES.

MOST PEOPLE ONLY UNDERSTAND THE ADVANTAGES OF USEFULNESS; VERY FEW UNDERSTAND THE BENEFITS OF USELESSNESS.

THE FAMOUS WAR STRATEGISTS, SHANG YANG, WU QI, SU QIN, AND ZHANG YI, WERE VERY INTELLIGENT MEN, BUT NONE OF THEM DIED A NATURAL DEATH. SOMETIMES INTELLIGENCE IS THE MEANS THAT TAKES ONE'S OWN LIFE.

魯有兀者叔山無趾，踵見仲尼。仲尼曰：「子不謹，前既犯患若是矣。雖今來，何及矣！」無趾曰：「吾唯不知務而輕用吾身，吾是以亡足。今吾來也，猶有尊足者存，吾是以務全之也。夫天無不覆，地無不載，吾以夫子為天地，安知夫子之猶若是也！」孔子曰：「丘則陋矣。夫子胡不入乎，請講以所聞！」無趾出。孔子曰：「弟子勉之！夫無趾，兀者也，猶務學以復補前行之惡，而況全德之人乎！」

61

仲尼曰：「丘也嘗使於楚矣，適見𤳊子食於其死母者，少焉眴若皆棄之而走。不見己焉爾，不得類焉爾。所愛其母者，非愛其形也，愛使其形者也。」

BODY
AND
SPIRIT

ONCE WHEN I WAS IN CHU, I SAW A LITTER OF PIGLETS BEING SUCKLED BY THEIR MOTHER.

ALL OF A SUDDEN, THE MOTHER ROLLED UP HER EYES AND DIED,

AND THE PIGLETS RAN AWAY IN FRIGHT.

ALTHOUGH THE PIGLETS LOVED THEIR MOTHER, IT WASN'T HER BODY THAT THEY LOVED, IT WAS THAT WHICH ANIMATED HER BODY.

THE BODY OF A LIVING SOW AND A NEWLY DEAD SOW LOOK THE SAME, BUT THE SPIRIT IS COMPLETELY DIFFERENT.

惠子謂莊子曰：「人故無情乎？」莊子曰：「然。」惠子曰：「人而無情，何以謂之人？」莊子曰：「道與之貌，天與之形，惡得不謂之人？」惠子曰：「既謂之人，惡得無情？」莊子曰：「是非吾所謂情也。吾所謂無情者，言人之不以好惡內傷其身，常因自然而不益生也。」惠子曰：「不益生，何以有其身？」莊子曰：「道與之貌，天與之形，以好惡內傷其身。今子外乎子之神，勞乎子之精，倚樹而吟，據槁梧而瞑。天選子之形，子以堅白鳴！」

CHAPTER 6

The Grand Master

WHAT IS A GENUINE PERSON?

ONLY A GENUINE PERSON CAN HAVE GENUINE WISDOM.

THE GENUINE PEOPLE OF OLD WERE NOT DISCOURAGED BY FAILURE, WERE NOT PROUD OF SUCCESS, AND DID NOT SCHEME FOR THINGS.

THEY DID NOT REGRET MISSED OPPORTUNITIES, AND WHEN THEY SUCCESSFULLY GRASPED OPPORTUNITY, THEY WERE NOT CONCEITED ABOUT IT.

ON MOUNTAIN PEAKS, THEY DIDN'T SHIVER.

IN WATER, THEY DIDN'T FEEL WET.

AND IN FIRE, THEY DIDN'T FEEL HOT.

ONLY WISDOM SUCH AS THIS CAN ATTAIN TO THE REALM OF THE DAO.

道

NOT JOYFUL AT BIRTH, NOT REFUSING DEATH; GLADLY ACCEPTING THINGS AS THEY HAPPEN; NOT USING THE INTELLECT TO HARM THE DAO; NOT CONTRIVING TO ASSIST NATURE— THIS IS A GENUINE PERSON!

CHAPTER 6
THE GRAND MASTER

且有真人而後有真知。何謂真人？古之真人，不逆寡，不雄成，不謨士。若然者，過而弗悔，當而不自得也。若然者，登高不慄，入水不濡，入火不熱。是知之能登假於道也若此。

死生，命也，其有夜旦之常，天也。人之有所不得與，皆物之情也。彼特以天為父而身猶愛之，而況其卓乎！人特以有君為愈乎己，而身猶死之，而況其真乎！

THE DAO IS HIGHER THAN HEAVEN

ALIVE

DEAD

BIRTH AND DEATH ARE DUE TO FATE, JUST AS NIGHT AND DAY ARE DUE TO THE HEAVENS—THEY ARE NOT THINGS THAT PEOPLE CAN ALTER, SO THERE IS NO REASON TO GET ATTACHED TO THEM.

PEOPLE JUST THINK THAT HEAVEN GAVE THEM LIFE, AND SO THEY RESPECT AND LOVE HEAVEN LIKE A FATHER...

BUT WHAT ABOUT THE DAO THAT IS A LEVEL HIGHER THAN HEAVEN?

PEOPLE THINK THAT THEIR SOVEREIGN HAS A HIGHER POSITION THAN THEM, SO THEY ARE WILLING TO DIE FOR HIM OUT OF LOYALTY...

BUT WHAT ABOUT THE DAO THAT HOLDS AN EVEN HIGHER POSITION?

A GENUINE PERSON DOES NOT BOAST ABOUT SUCCESS, DOES NOT COMPLAIN ABOUT HAVING TOO LITTLE, AND DOES NOT SEEK A GOOD REPUTATION. HE TAKES THE DAO AS A MASTER TO BE EMULATED.

MINDLESS OF EACH OTHER

WHEN A RIVER OR LAKE DRIES UP...

THE FISH ARE TRAPPED ON LAND AND WET EACH OTHER WITH THEIR MUCUS, JUST TRYING TO STAY ALIVE...

HERE, MOISTEN YOURSELF WITH THIS SO YOU DON'T DRY OUT.

OH, THANK YOU! YOU'RE SO BENEVOLENT AND RIGHTEOUS...

WHAT'S BETTER THAN THIS IS TO HAVE THE RIVERS AND LAKES FULL OF WATER AND THE FISH LEISURELY SWIMMING ABOUT COMPLETELY CAREFREE AND MINDLESS OF EACH OTHER.

BENEVOLENCE IS, AFTER ALL, LIMITED. WHEN PEOPLE NEED TO USE BENEVOLENCE TO HELP EACH OTHER, THE WORLD HAS ALREADY TURNED BAD. NATURE'S LOVE IS LIMITLESS, SO WE SHOULD BE MINDLESS OF EACH OTHER IN NATURE, JUST LIKE THE FISH IN RIVERS AND LAKES.

泉涸，魚相與處於陸，相呴以濕，相濡以沫，不如相忘於江湖。與其譽堯而非桀也，不如兩忘而化其道。

夫大塊載我以形，勞我以生，佚我以老，息我以死……。故聖人將遊於物之所不得遯而皆存。善夭善老，善始善終，人猶效之，又況萬物之所係，而一化之所待乎！

NATURE THE SUPERHERO

NATURE IS LIKE A SUPERHERO, ITS LIMITLESS STRENGTH CONTINUALLY PULSING.

NATURE GAVE ME MY BODY,

GAVE ME VITALITY SO THAT I CAN WORK HARD,

GAVE ME AGE SO THAT I CAN GROW OLD IN EASE AND COMFORT,

AND GAVE ME DEATH SO THAT I CAN HAVE EVERLASTING PEACE.

NATURE IS CONSTANTLY CHANGING, AND PEOPLE HAVE TO ACKNOWLEDGE AND ADAPT TO THESE CHANGES. THIS WAY, REACTIONS OF DELIGHT AND FEAR WILL DISSIPATE, AND THE DISTINCTION BETWEEN LIFE AND DEATH WILL LOSE ITS SIGNIFICANCE.

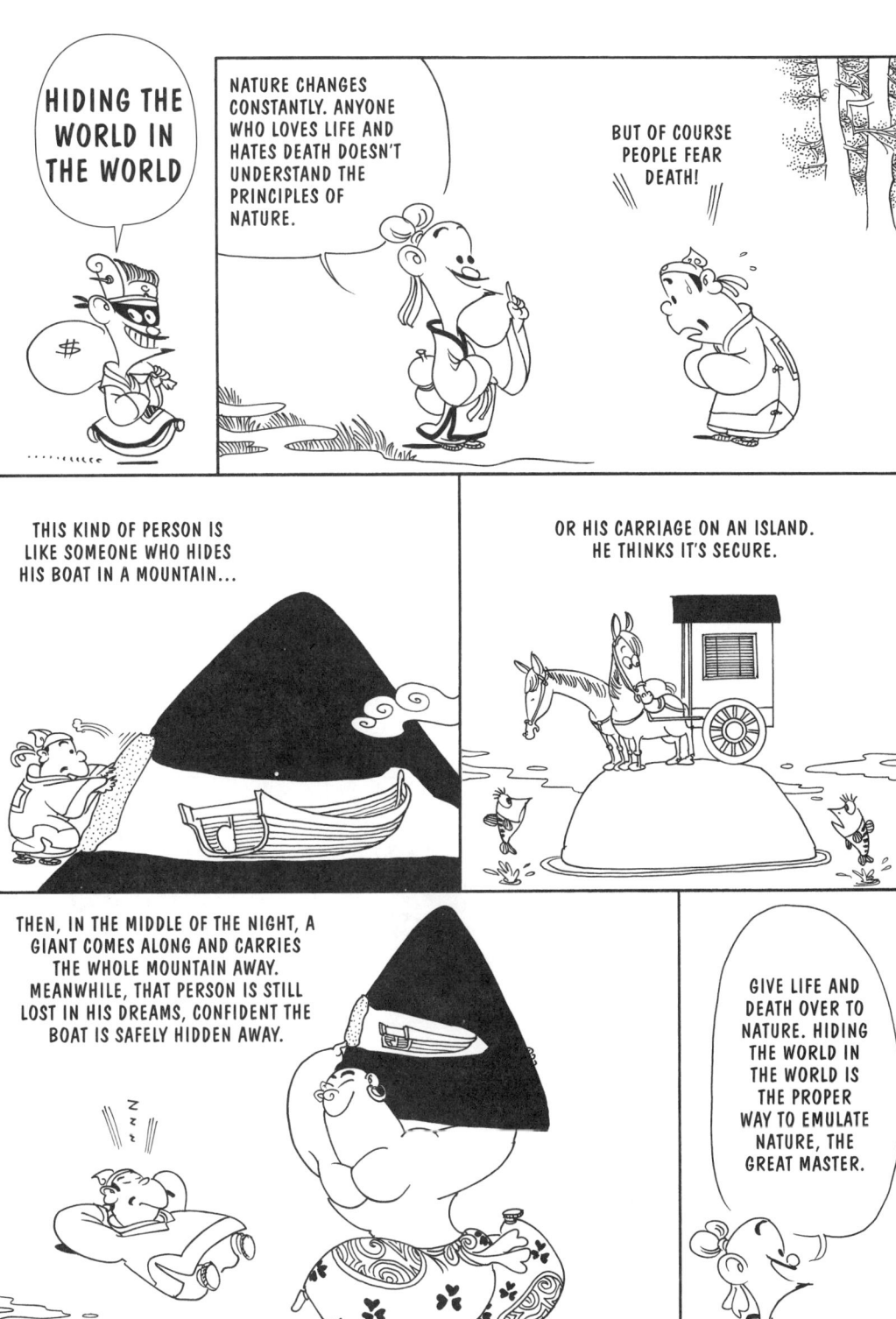

HIDING THE WORLD IN THE WORLD

NATURE CHANGES CONSTANTLY. ANYONE WHO LOVES LIFE AND HATES DEATH DOESN'T UNDERSTAND THE PRINCIPLES OF NATURE.

BUT OF COURSE PEOPLE FEAR DEATH!

THIS KIND OF PERSON IS LIKE SOMEONE WHO HIDES HIS BOAT IN A MOUNTAIN...

OR HIS CARRIAGE ON AN ISLAND. HE THINKS IT'S SECURE.

THEN, IN THE MIDDLE OF THE NIGHT, A GIANT COMES ALONG AND CARRIES THE WHOLE MOUNTAIN AWAY. MEANWHILE, THAT PERSON IS STILL LOST IN HIS DREAMS, CONFIDENT THE BOAT IS SAFELY HIDDEN AWAY.

GIVE LIFE AND DEATH OVER TO NATURE. HIDING THE WORLD IN THE WORLD IS THE PROPER WAY TO EMULATE NATURE, THE GREAT MASTER.

夫藏舟於壑，藏山於澤，謂之固矣。然而夜半有力者負之而走，昧者不知也。藏小大有宜，猶有所遯。若

夫藏天下於天下而不得所遯，是恆物之大情也。

69

子貢曰：「然則夫子何方之依？」曰：「丘，天之戮民也。雖然，吾與汝共之。」子貢曰：「敢問其方。」孔子曰：「魚相造乎水，人相造乎道。相造乎水者，穿池而養給；相造乎道者，無事而生定。故曰，魚相忘乎江湖，人相忘乎道術。」

意而子見許由。許由曰：「堯何以資汝？」意而子曰：「堯謂我：『汝必躬服仁義而明言是非。』」許由曰：

「而奚來為軹？夫堯既已黥汝以仁義，而劓汝以是非矣，汝將何以遊夫遙蕩恣睢轉徙之塗乎？」意而子曰：「雖

然，吾願遊於其藩。」許由曰：「不然。夫盲者無以與乎眉目顏色之好，瞽者無以與乎青黃黼黻之觀。」

意而子曰：「夫無莊之失其美，據梁之失其力，黃帝之亡其知，皆在鑪捶之間耳。庸詎知夫造物者之不息我黥而補我劓，使我乘成以隨先生邪？」許由曰：「噫！未可知也。我為汝言其大略。吾師乎！吾師乎！齏萬物而不為義，澤及萬世而不為仁，長於上古而不為老，覆載天地刻彫眾形而不為巧，此所遊已。」

顔回曰：「回益矣。」仲尼曰：「何謂也？」曰：「回忘仁義矣。」曰：「可矣，猶未也。」他日，復見，曰：「回益矣。」曰：「何謂也？」曰：「回忘禮樂矣。」曰：「可矣，猶未也。」

73

他日，復見，曰：「回益矣。」曰：「何謂也？」曰：「回坐忘矣。」仲尼蹴然曰：「何謂坐忘？」顏回曰：「墮枝體，黜聰明，離形去知，同於大通，此謂坐忘。」仲尼曰：「同則無好也，化則無常也。而果其賢乎！丘也請從而後也。」

ZISANG QUESTIONS HIS FATE

ZIYU AND ZISANG WERE GOOD FRIENDS.

ONCE WHEN IT HAD RAINED FOR MORE THAN TEN DAYS IN A ROW, ZIYU TOOK SOME FOOD AND WENT TO SEE ZISANG.

MOTHER! FATHER! HEAVEN! OH! WOE IS ME!

WHAT'S WRONG?

I'M SICK, AND THESE PAST FEW DAYS I'VE BEEN THINKING...

WHO MADE ME SO WRETCHED? WAS IT MY PARENTS? WAS IT NATURE?

NO ONE WISHED THIS UPON ME, AND YET HERE I AM. OH, MY WRETCHEDNESS MUST BE FATE!

THOSE THINGS THAT HAPPEN BY CHANCE ARE CALLED FATE. BEING BORN A PRINCE OR A PAUPER IS SOMETHING WE CANNOT CONTROL, SO WE MUST ACCEPT OUR FATE AND FIND SOLACE IN OUR FRIEND, THE DAO.

CHAPTER 6
THE GRAND MASTER

子輿與子桑友，而霖雨十日。子輿曰：「子桑殆病矣！」裹飯而往食之。至子桑之門，則若歌若哭，鼓琴曰：「父邪！母邪！天乎！人乎！」有不任其聲而趨舉其詩焉。子輿入，曰：「子之歌詩，何故若是？」曰：「吾思夫使我至此極者而弗得也。父母豈欲吾貧哉？天無私覆，地無私載，天地豈私貧我哉？求其為之者而不得也。然而至此極者，命也夫！」

75

肩吾見狂接輿。狂接輿曰：「日中始何以語女？」肩吾曰：「告我君人者以己出經式義度，人孰敢不聽而化諸！」狂接輿曰：「是欺德也，其於治天下也，猶涉海鑿河而使蚊負山也。」

DIGGING A HOLE IN THE OCEAN FLOOR

ONE DAY WHEN JIAN WU WENT TO SEE CRAZY JIEYU, JIEYU ASKED:

WHAT DID RI ZHONGSHI SAY TO YOU?

HE SAID ONLY PEOPLE WHO ARE REGULATED ACCORDING TO LEGAL AND MORAL CODES WILL SUBMIT AND BE CIVIL.

I BEG TO DIFFER. THAT METHOD OF GOVERNING IS LIKE TRYING TO DIG A HOLE IN THE OCEAN FLOOR

OR LIKE TELLING A MOSQUITO TO CARRY A MOUNTAIN ON ITS BACK.

LAWS AND CUSTOMS ARE TEMPORAL, OR TRANSITIONAL. IF UNIVERSAL PEACE IS TO BE ACHIEVED, WE MUST FOLLOW THE LAWS OF NATURE, OR THE DAO.

無為名尸，無為謀府，無為事任，無為知主。體盡無窮，而遊無朕；盡其所受乎天，而無見得，亦虛而已。

至人之用心若鏡，不將不迎，應而不藏，故能勝物而不傷。

THE MIND IS LIKE A MIRROR

DO NOT PURSUE FAME,
DO NOT OCCUPY YOURSELF WITH SCHEMING,
DO NOT CONCERN YOURSELF WITH TRIFLES,
DO NOT STRIVE FOR GREAT WISDOM.

EXPERIENCE THE BOUNDLESS AND WANDER IN INFINITY. USE WHAT NATURE HAS GIVEN YOU WITHOUT BOASTING ABOUT ACHIEVEMENTS. JUST BE EMPTY.

THE PERFECT PERSON'S MIND IS LIKE A MIRROR, ACCEPTING THINGS AS THEY COME AND GO, NEITHER WELCOMING THEM IN, NOR SHOWING THEM OUT,

RESPONDING TO THINGS NATURALLY WITHOUT STORING THEM UP. THEREFORE, THE PERFECT PERSON IS ABLE TO OVERCOME MATERIAL THINGS AND NOT BE HARMED BY THEM.

THE PERFECT PERSON TREATS THE MIND LIKE A MIRROR. WHEN SOMETHING HAPPENS, RESPOND, AND WHEN IT'S OVER, EMPTY YOUR MIND OF IT. GENUINELY APPRECIATE EVERY MOMENT OF LIFE.

南海之帝為儵，北海之帝為忽，中央之帝為渾沌。儵與忽時相與遇於渾沌之地，渾沌待之甚善。儵與忽謀報渾沌之德，曰：「人皆有七竅以視聽食息，此獨無有，嘗試鑿之。」日鑿一竅，七日而渾沌死。

CHAPTER 8
FUSED TOES

駢拇枝指，出乎性哉！而侈於德。附贅縣疣，出乎形哉！而侈於性。多方乎仁義而用之者，列於五藏哉！而非道德之正也。是故駢於足者，連無用之肉也；枝於手者，樹無用之指也；多方駢枝於五藏之情者，淫僻於仁義之行，而多方於聰明之用也。

長者不為有餘，短者不為不足。是故鳧脛雖短，續之則憂；鶴脛雖長，斷之則悲。故性長非所斷，性短非所續，無所去憂也。意仁義其非人情乎！彼仁人何其多憂也？

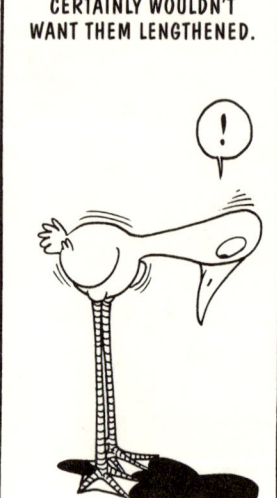

GREAT CONFUSION ALTERS ONE'S NATURE

A MINOR CONFUSION WILL ALTER ONE'S SENSE OF DIRECTION, BUT A GREAT CONFUSION WILL ALTER ONE'S ORIGINAL NATURE. SINCE THE THREE DYNASTIES PERIOD, THERE HAS BEEN NO ONE WHO DIDN'T ALTER THEIR ORIGINAL NATURE WITH EXTERNAL THINGS.

PETTY PEOPLE SACRIFICE THEMSELVES FOR PROFIT,

FAME IS FOR THE BIRDS. PROFIT IS WHAT COUNTS.

OFFICIALS SACRIFICE THEMSELVES FOR FAME,

NOBLEMEN SACRIFICE THEMSELVES FOR FAMILY,

FOR MY COUNTRY AND MY FAMILY, LIFE IS NOT TO BE CHERISHED.

AND SAGES SACRIFICE THEMSELVES FOR THE WHOLE LAND.

THESE PEOPLE ARE ALL DIFFERENT, WITH DIFFERENT TITLES AND DIFFERENT STATIONS IN LIFE, BUT THEIR HARMING OF THEIR ORIGINAL NATURES AND SACRIFICING THEMSELVES IS THE SAME. THEY ARE ALL CONFUSED.

CHAPTER 8
FUSED TOES

夫小惑易方，大惑易性。何以知其然邪？… 故嘗試論之，自三代以下者，天下莫不以物易其性矣。小人則以身殉利，士則以身殉名，大夫則以身殉家，聖人則以身殉天下。故此數子者，事業不同，名聲異號，其於傷性以身為殉，一也。

81

臧與穀，二人相與牧羊而俱亡其羊。問臧奚事，則挾筴讀書，問穀奚事，則博塞以遊。二人者，事業不同，其於亡羊均也。伯夷死名於首陽之下，盜跖死利於東陵之上，二人者，所死不同，其於殘生傷性均也，奚必伯夷之是而盜跖之非乎！天下盡殉也。彼其所殉仁義也，則俗謂之君子；其所殉貨財也，則俗謂之小人。其殉一也，則有君子焉，有小人焉；若其殘生損性，則盜跖亦伯夷已，又惡取君子小人於其間哉！

THE LOST GOAT

TWO MEN NAMED ZANG AND GU WERE TAKING CARE OF THEIR GOATS ONE DAY WHEN:

I LOST A GOAT!

I DID, TOO!

IT JUST WALKED AWAY WHILE I WAS SITTING HERE STUDYING!

I WAS GAMBLING WHEN MINE WALKED AWAY!

ALTHOUGH ZANG AND GU WERE DOING TWO ENTIRELY DIFFERENT THINGS, THE FINAL RESULT OF BOTH WAS A LOST GOAT.

SOME PEOPLE THROW THEIR LIVES AWAY IN PURSUIT OF FAME. OTHERS IN THE PURSUIT OF RICHES.

STATESMEN THROW THEIR LIVES AWAY TRYING TO SAVE THE COUNTRY, AND SAGES THROW THEIR LIVES AWAY TRYING TO SAVE THE WORLD.

THE REASONS MAY BE DIFFERENT, BUT, IN THE END, THEIR LIVES ARE WASTED.

IT DOESN'T MATTER WHAT EXCUSES ARE MADE, DEFYING NATURE IS THROWING ONE'S LIFE AWAY, AND THAT JUST CREATES MORE CONFUSION.

THE HORSE TRAINER'S TRANSGRESSIONS

A HORSE'S HOOVES CAN STAND ON FROST AND SNOW, AND ITS FUR CAN PROTECT IT FROM COLD WINDS.

IT EATS GRASS AND DRINKS WATER; THEN, STRETCHING ITS LEGS, IT LEAPS INTO THE AIR. THIS IS THE ORIGINAL NATURE OF HORSES.

IF YOU WERE TO BUILD A LUXURIOUS MANSION FOR IT, THE HORSE WOULD SEE IT AS USELESS.

BUT EVER SINCE THE GREAT HORSE TRAINER BO LE, THE SITUATION HAS CHANGED...

I'M THE BEST HORSE TRAINER EVER!

馬，蹄可以踐霜雪，毛可以禦風寒，齕草飲水，翹足而陸，此馬之真性也。雖有義臺路寢，無所用之。及至伯樂，曰：「我善治馬。」

83

燒之，剔之，刻之，雒之，連之以羈馽，編之以皁棧，馬之死者十二三矣；飢之，渴之，馳之，驟之，整之，齊之，前有橛飾之患，而後有鞭筴之威，而馬之死者已過半矣……。此亦治天下者之過也。

THE HARM OF MORALITY

IN HIGHEST ANTIQUITY, PEOPLE LIVED CONTENTEDLY, OBLIVIOUS TO WHAT THEY WERE DOING OR WHERE THEY WERE GOING.

COMPLETELY AT EASE, THEY WALKED AROUND WITH PROTRUDING BELLIES AND WANDERED WHERE THEY WOULD.

THEN SAGES CAME ALONG, CONTRIVING PROPRIETY AND MUSIC TO RECTIFY PEOPLE'S APPEARANCES, AND PROMOTING BENEVOLENCE AND RIGHTEOUSNESS TO TRANSFORM THEIR ORIGINAL NATURES.

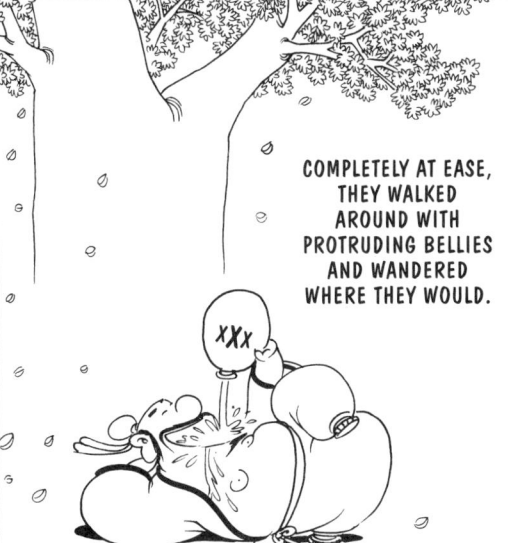

FROM THEN ON, PEOPLE BECAME OVERCONFIDENT IN THEIR PREFERENCES AND KNOWLEDGE AND RELENTLESSLY PURSUED THEIR OWN PERSONAL BENEFIT.

WITH THE DESTRUCTION OF THE DAO, MORALITY ARISES. WITH THE COMING OF INTELLIGENCE, DECEPTION AND HYPOCRISY ARISE. IN HIGHEST ANTIQUITY, PEOPLE WERE IGNORANT YET HONEST. THEY DIDN'T EVEN KNOW WHAT DECEPTION AND HYPOCRISY WERE, SO WHY WOULD THEY NEED MORALITY?

夫赫胥氏之時，民居不知所為，行不知所之，含哺而熙，鼓腹而遊，民能以此矣。及至聖人，屈折禮樂以匡天下之形，縣跂仁義以慰天下之心，而民乃始踶跂好知，爭歸於利，不可止也。此亦聖人之過也。

將為胠篋探囊發匱之盜而為守備，則必攝緘縢，固扃鐍，此世俗之所謂知也。然而巨盜至，則負匱揭篋擔囊而趨，唯恐緘縢扃鐍之不固也。然則鄉之所謂知者，不乃為大盜積者也？故嘗試論之，世俗所謂知者，有不為大盜積者乎？所謂聖者，有不為大盜守者乎？何以知其然邪？

THEFT PREVENTION

PEOPLE NORMALLY LOCK THEIR VALUABLES UP IN A CHEST, THINKING IT'S THE BEST METHOD OF PREVENTING THEFT.

NO THIEF WILL EVER OPEN THAT LOCK.

THEN ONE EVENING A BURGLAR COMES ALONG...

I SEE EVERYTHING IS NEATLY PACKED FOR ME!

I'LL JUST TAKE THE WHOLE THING.

AND ON THE WAY HOME, HIS ONLY WORRY IS THAT THE LOCK MIGHT NOT BE SECURE ENOUGH!

COMMON INGENUITY OFTEN INVITES UNINTENDED HARM. RULERS CREATED PROPRIETY AND LAWS TO PREVENT CRIMES, BUT CRIMINALS (OFTEN THE RULERS THEMSELVES) SIMPLY USURP THEM FOR THEIR OWN PROTECTION.

跖之徒問於跖曰：「盜亦有道乎？」跖曰：「何適而無有道邪！」夫妄意室中之藏，聖也；入先，勇也；出後，義也：；

跖不得聖人之道不行，天下之善人少而不善人多，則聖人之利天下也少而害天下也多。

知可否，知也；分均，仁也。五者不備而能成大盜者，天下未之有也。由是觀之，善人不得聖人之道不立，

GOOD WINE, BAD WINE

ONCE, THE STATE OF CHU THREW A MAGNIFICENT FEAST AND INVITED NOBLEMEN FROM ALL OVER THE LAND. THE STATES OF LU AND ZHAO BROUGHT GIFTS OF THEIR MOST FAMOUS WINE.

ZHAO
LU
ZHAO

I HEAR THAT ZHAO WINE IS OF A MOST EXCELLENT VINTAGE. MAY I HAVE A TASTE?

SORRY!

ZHAO

YOUR MAJESTY, ZHAO INTENTIONALLY SENT US INFERIOR QUALITY WINE!

THOSE SCOUNDRELS!

BLAST IT!

THIS CURT REJECTION ANGERED THE CHU WINE MINISTER, WHO THEN SWITCHED THE ZHAO WINE WITH THE INFERIOR LU WINE.

ZHAO
LU

AFTER THE FEAST, THE CHU KING SENT OUT AN ARMY, WHICH SURROUNDED AND CAPTURED THE CAPITAL OF ZHAO.

CHU

WINE CAN BRING NOT ONLY HAPPINESS AND GOOD TIMES, IT CAN ALSO BRING DEATH AND DESTRUCTION.

XXX

CHAPTER 10
STOLEN CHESTS

故曰，脣竭則齒寒，魯酒薄而邯鄲圍，聖人生而大盜起。掊擊聖人，縱舍盜賊，而天下始治矣。夫川竭而谷虛，丘夷而淵實。聖人已死，則大盜不起，天下平而無故矣。

許慎注《淮南子》云：「楚會諸侯。魯趙俱獻酒于楚王。魯酒薄而趙酒厚。楚之主酒吏求酒于趙，趙不與。吏怒，乃以趙厚酒易魯薄酒奏之。楚王以趙酒薄故圍邯鄲也。」

89

黃帝立為天子十九年，令行天下，聞廣成子在於空同之上，故往見之，曰：「……吾欲取天地之精，以佐五穀，以養民人，吾又欲官陰陽，以遂群生，為之奈何？」廣成子曰：「……所欲官者，物之殘也。自而治天下，雲氣不待族而雨，草木不待黃而落，日月之光益以荒矣。而佞人之心翦翦者，又奚足以語至道！」黃帝退，捐天下，築特室，席白茅，間居三月，復往邀之……。曰：「……治身奈何而可以長久？」廣成子蹶然而起，曰：「……無視無聽，抱神以靜，形將自正。必靜必清，無勞女形，無搖女精，乃可以長生。目無所見，耳無所聞，心無所知，女神將守形，形乃長生。慎女內，閉女外，多知為敗……。我守其一以處其和。」

THE YELLOW EMPEROR QUESTIONS GUANGCHENGZI

WHEN THE YELLOW EMPEROR HAD BEEN REIGNING FOR NINETEEN YEARS AND HAD BROUGHT CIVILIZATION TO THE LAND, HE HEARD ABOUT AN ENLIGHTENED MASTER NAMED GUANGCHENGZI. OUT OF CURIOSITY, THE EMPEROR WENT TO SEE HIM.

I WANT TO USE THE VITALITY OF NATURE TO HARMONIZE THE YIN AND THE YANG; THIS WILL BRING UNPRECEDENTED HARVESTS. I WANT TO HELP MY PEOPLE CULTIVATE THEIR ORIGINAL NATURES ...

YOU SAY YOU WANT TO USE THE VITALITY OF THE DAO TO ENHANCE THE NATURAL PROCESSES? THIS WILL ONLY DESTROY THEM. DON'T YOU UNDERSTAND THAT TO USE OUR INTELLECT TO CHANGE THINGS ONLY MAKES MATTERS WORSE?

UPON HEARING THIS, THE EMPEROR'S PASSION TURNED TO DUST AND HE IMMEDIATELY ABDICATED. HE LEFT THE WORLD BEHIND AND WENT TO LIVE BY HIMSELF IN A GRASS HUT. HE STAYED THERE IN PEACE AND SOLITUDE FOR THREE MONTHS.

HOW SHOULD I GOVERN MY BODY THAT I MAY LIVE A LONG LIFE?

THE DAO IS CHAOTIC, NEITHER BRIGHT NOR DARK.

DON'T SEE WITH YOUR EYES, DON'T HEAR WITH YOUR EARS, DON'T THINK WITH YOUR MIND, EMBRACE THE PRIMAL ONE, NO KNOWLEDGE, NO SELF, GO WITH NATURE, PARTICIPATE IN NATURE, BE ONE WITH NATURE, AND A LONG LIFE WILL COME NATURALLY.

NATURE'S FRIEND

THERE IS A KIND OF SAGE WHO EMULATES THE WISDOM OF NATURE.

HIS METHODS OF TEACHING AND TRANSFORMING ARE LIKE THE RELATIONSHIP OF A FORM AND ITS SHADOW...

...A SOUND AND ITS ECHO. WHERE THERE'S A QUESTION, THERE'S AN ANSWER; WHERE THERE'S AN ACTION, THERE'S A REACTION.

HELLO!

HELLO...

FROM INSIDE OUT, HE COOPERATES WITH NATURE. WHEN HE IS AT REST, THERE IS NO SOUND.

WHEN HE MOVES, HE LEAVES NO TRACE. THEREFORE, HE IS ABLE TO BRING THOSE WHO ARE MUDDLED AND CONFUSED BACK TO THE NATURAL DAO.

THOSE WHO FOCUS ON THE SELF AS CORPOREAL FORM HAVE OFTEN BEEN THOUGHT TO BE THE WISE ONES, BUT THE PERSON WHO IS ABLE TO SEE THE NO-SELF IS THE TRUE COMPANION OF NATURE.

ONLY THE SELFLESS PERSON CAN LIVE UP TO THE STANDARDS OF NATURE BECAUSE YOUR BODY IS JUST ONE TEMPORARY FORM IN NATURE'S CONSTANTLY CHANGING PROCESS. SELFISHNESS IS TRYING TO HANG ONTO WHAT YOU HAVE.

大人之教，若形之於影，聲之於嚮。有問而應之，盡其所懷，為天下配。處乎無嚮，行乎無方。挈汝適復之撓撓，以遊無端；出入無旁，與日無始；頌論形軀，合乎大同，大同而無己。無己，惡乎得有有！睹有者，昔之君子；睹無者，天地之友。

CHAPTER 12
HEAVEN AND EARTH

黄帝遊乎赤水之北，登乎崑崙之丘而南望，還歸，遺其玄珠。使知索之而不得，使離朱索之而不得，

CHI GOU, THE GREAT DEBATER, SEARCHED, BUT HE COULDN'T FIND IT, EITHER.

IMAGELESS, WHY DON'T YOU GO LOOK FOR IT?

YES, YOUR MAJESTY.

FINALLY, IT WAS IMAGELESS WHO FOUND THE MYSTERIOUS PEARL.

HERE IT IS, YOUR MAJESTY.

HOW STRANGE THAT ONLY IMAGELESS WAS ABLE TO FIND THE PEARL!

THE DAO CANNOT BE OBTAINED BY WAY OF KNOWLEDGE, THE SENSES, OR DEBATE. ONLY NON-INTENTION AND NON-AFFECTATION CAN FIND IT—BECAUSE THE DAO IS A REALM BEYOND THE INTELLECT AND THE SENSES.

使喫詬索之而不得也。乃使象罔，象罔得之。黃帝曰：「異哉！象罔乃可以得之乎？」

93

天道運而無所積，故萬物成；帝道運而無所積，故天下歸；聖道運而無所積，故海內服。明於天，通於聖，六通四辟於帝王之德者，其自為也，昧然無不靜者矣。聖人之靜也，非曰靜也善，故靜也；萬物無足以鐃心者，故靜也。

THE HEAVENLY DAO

THE HEAVENLY DAO COURSES WITHOUT END, AND THUS THE MYRIAD THINGS ARISE.

THE IMPERIAL DAO COURSES WITHOUT END, AND THUS THE ENTIRE LAND PAYS ALLEGIANCE.

THE SAGELY DAO COURSES WITHOUT END, AND THUS ALL WITHIN THE FOUR SEAS PAY HOMAGE.

THE COURSING OF THE DAO IS UNENDING, AND IN THE NATURAL REALM THE MYRIAD THINGS MOVE ABOUT OF THEIR OWN ACCORD. THE SAGE EMULATES THE DAO AND LOOKS AFTER THE MYRIAD THINGS WITH A SERENE MIND.

昔者舜問於堯曰：「天王之用心何如？」堯曰：「吾不敖無告，不廢窮民，苦死者，嘉孺子而哀婦人。此吾所以用心已。」舜曰：「美則美矣，而未大也。」堯曰：「然則何如？」舜曰：「天德而出寧，日月照而四時行，若晝夜之有經，雲行而雨施矣。」堯曰：「膠膠擾擾乎！子，天之合也。我，人之合也。」夫天地者，古之所大也，而黃帝堯舜之所共美也。故古之王天下者，奚為哉？天地而已矣。

桓公讀書於堂上。輪扁斲輪於堂下，釋椎鑿而上，問桓公曰：「敢問，公之所讀者何言邪？」公曰：「聖人之言也。」曰：「聖人在乎？」公曰：「已死矣。」曰：「然則君之所讀者，古人之糟魄已夫！」桓公曰：「寡人讀書，輪人安得議乎！有說則可，無說則死。」輪扁曰：「臣也以臣之事觀之。斲輪，徐則甘而不固，疾則苦而不入。

THE SECRET TO WHEELMAKING IS A CHISEL THAT IS NEITHER LEISURELY NOR FAST, BUT ONE THAT MOVES EXACTLY AS YOU WISH IT.

I CAN EXPLAIN THIS TO MY SON, BUT I CAN'T PASS ON THE SKILL TO HIM, AND THAT IS WHY AT SEVENTY YEARS OLD, I AM STILL MAKING WHEELS.

SO YOU SEE, THE WISDOM OF ANCIENT SAGES CAN'T NECESSARILY BE PASSED DOWN, AND THAT'S WHY I SAY THE BOOK YOU'RE READING IS MERELY THE DREGS OF A DEAD MAN.

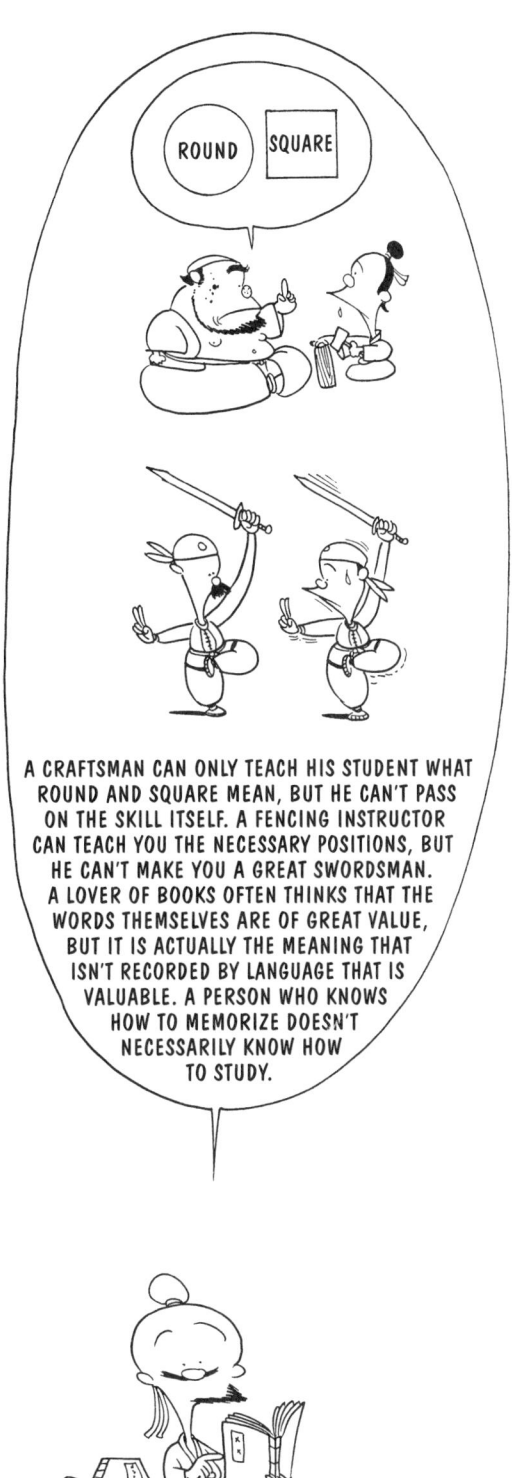

ROUND SQUARE

A CRAFTSMAN CAN ONLY TEACH HIS STUDENT WHAT ROUND AND SQUARE MEAN, BUT HE CAN'T PASS ON THE SKILL ITSELF. A FENCING INSTRUCTOR CAN TEACH YOU THE NECESSARY POSITIONS, BUT HE CAN'T MAKE YOU A GREAT SWORDSMAN. A LOVER OF BOOKS OFTEN THINKS THAT THE WORDS THEMSELVES ARE OF GREAT VALUE, BUT IT IS ACTUALLY THE MEANING THAT ISN'T RECORDED BY LANGUAGE THAT IS VALUABLE. A PERSON WHO KNOWS HOW TO MEMORIZE DOESN'T NECESSARILY KNOW HOW TO STUDY.

不徐不疾，得之於手，而應於心，口不能言，有數存焉於其間。臣不能以喻臣之子，臣之子亦不能受之於臣，是以行年七十而老斲輪。古之人與其不可傳也死矣，然則君之所讀者，古人之糟魄已夫！」

天其運乎？地其處乎？日月其爭於所乎？孰主張是？孰維綱是？孰居無事推而行是？意者其有機緘而不得已邪？意者其運轉而不能自止邪？雲者為雨乎？雨者為雲乎？孰隆施是？孰居無事淫樂而勸是？風起北方，一西一東，有上彷徨，孰嘘吸是？孰居無事而披拂是？敢問何故？

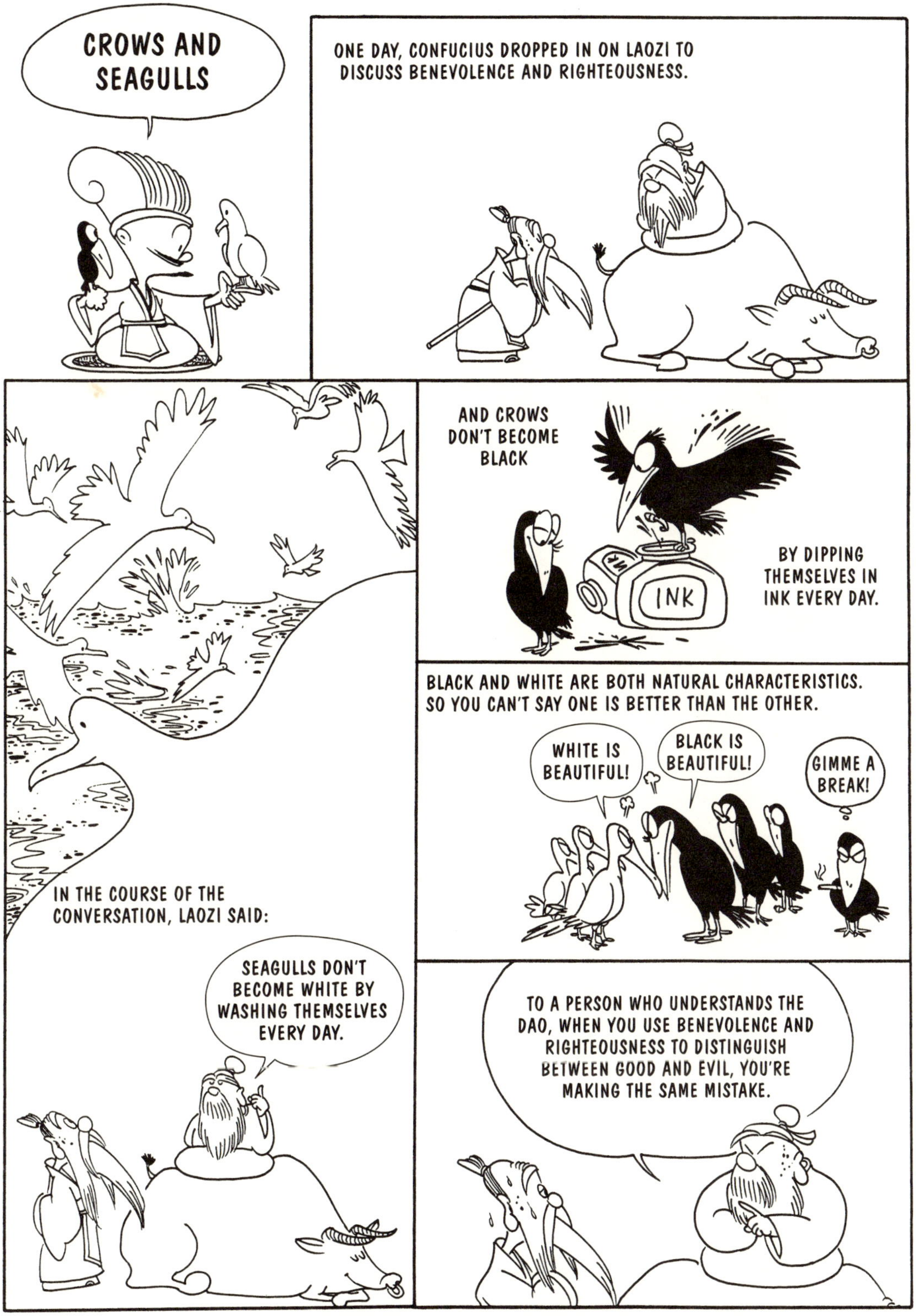

CROWS AND SEAGULLS
ONE DAY, CONFUCIUS DROPPED IN ON LAOZI TO DISCUSS BENEVOLENCE AND RIGHTEOUSNESS.
IN THE COURSE OF THE CONVERSATION, LAOZI SAID:
SEAGULLS DON'T BECOME WHITE BY WASHING THEMSELVES EVERY DAY.
AND CROWS DON'T BECOME BLACK
INK
BY DIPPING THEMSELVES IN INK EVERY DAY.
BLACK AND WHITE ARE BOTH NATURAL CHARACTERISTICS. SO YOU CAN'T SAY ONE IS BETTER THAN THE OTHER.
WHITE IS BEAUTIFUL!
BLACK IS BEAUTIFUL!
GIMME A BREAK!
TO A PERSON WHO UNDERSTANDS THE DAO, WHEN YOU USE BENEVOLENCE AND RIGHTEOUSNESS TO DISTINGUISH BETWEEN GOOD AND EVIL, YOU'RE MAKING THE SAME MISTAKE.

CHAPTER 14
THE MOVING SKY

孔子見老聃而語仁義。老聃曰：「夫播穅眯目，則天地四方易位矣；蚊虻噆膚，則通昔不寐矣。夫仁義憯然乃憤吾心，亂莫大焉。吾子使天下無失其朴，吾子亦放風而動，總德而立矣，又奚傑然若負建鼓而求亡子者邪？夫鵠不日浴而白，烏不日黔而黑。黑白之朴，不足以為辯；名譽之觀，不足以為廣。

孔子見老聃歸，三日不談。弟子問曰：「夫子見老聃，亦將何規哉？」孔子曰：「吾乃今於是乎見龍！龍，合而成體，散而成章，乘乎雲氣而養乎陰陽。予口張而不能嚍，予又何規老聃哉！」

CONFUCIUS SEES A DRAGON

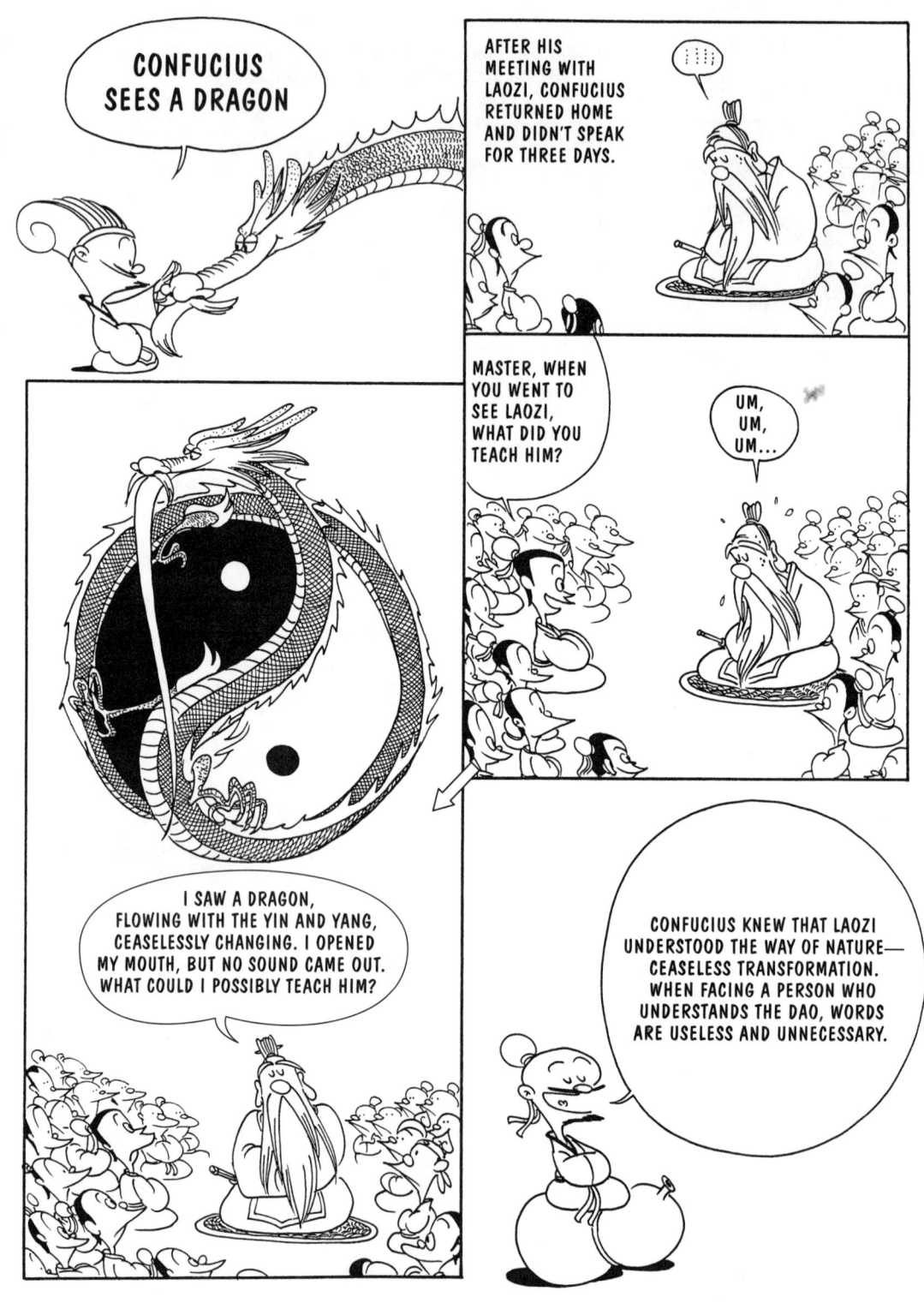

AFTER HIS MEETING WITH LAOZI, CONFUCIUS RETURNED HOME AND DIDN'T SPEAK FOR THREE DAYS.

MASTER, WHEN YOU WENT TO SEE LAOZI, WHAT DID YOU TEACH HIM?

UM, UM, UM...

I SAW A DRAGON, FLOWING WITH THE YIN AND YANG, CEASELESSLY CHANGING. I OPENED MY MOUTH, BUT NO SOUND CAME OUT. WHAT COULD I POSSIBLY TEACH HIM?

CONFUCIUS KNEW THAT LAOZI UNDERSTOOD THE WAY OF NATURE—CEASELESS TRANSFORMATION. WHEN FACING A PERSON WHO UNDERSTANDS THE DAO, WORDS ARE USELESS AND UNNECESSARY.

刻意尚行，離世異俗，高論怨誹，為亢而已矣，此山谷之士，非世之人，枯槁赴淵者之所好也。語仁義忠信，恭儉推讓，為脩而已矣；此平世之士，教誨之人，遊居學者之所好也。語大功，立大名，禮君臣，正上下，為治而已矣，此朝廷之士，尊主彊國之人，致功并兼者之所好也。

INDEPENDENT LEISURE

CURBING AMBITION AND ACTING SUPERIOR, SEEING ONESELF AS SPECIAL AND SEPARATE FROM THE WORLD, SERMONIZING AND BEMOANING THE EVILS OF THE WORLD—THESE ARE SIMPLY FOR SHOW AND ARE WHAT FOREST HERMITS, CYNICS, AND IDEALISTS LIKE TO DO.

DISCUSSING VIRTUES AND MORALITY, RESPECTING FRUGALITY, AND PROMOTING HUMILITY—THESE ARE JUST FOR DEVELOPING ONESELF AND ARE WHAT POLITICAL HOPEFULS, INSTRUCTORS, AND ITINERANT SCHOLARS LIKE TO DO.

DISCUSSING GREAT ACCOMPLISHMENTS, ESTABLISHING GREAT REPUTATIONS, MAINTAINING THE SOVEREIGN-VASSAL RELATIONSHIP, AND RECTIFYING THE SUPERIOR-INFERIOR RELATIONSHIPS—THESE ARE JUST FOR GOVERNING AND ARE WHAT COURT PATRONS, SYMPATHIZERS OF OPPRESSIVE REGIMES, AND COLONIALISTS LIKE TO DO.

就藪澤，處閒曠，釣魚閒處，無為而已矣；此江海之士，避世之人，間暇者之所好也。吹呴呼吸，吐故納新，熊經鳥申，為壽而已矣；此道引之士，養形之人，彭祖壽考者之所好也。若夫不刻意而高，無仁義而脩，無功名而治，無江海而閒，不道引而壽，無不忘也，無不有也，澹然無極而眾美從之。此天地之道，聖人之德也。

GOING TO MARSHES AND SWAMPS, LIVING IN WIDE OPEN SPACES, FISHING IN A QUIET SPOT—THESE ARE JUST FOR RELAXATION AND ARE WHAT PEOPLE OF THE SEA AND RIVERS, RECLUSES, AND PEOPLE OF LEISURE LIKE TO DO.

EXHALING AND INHALING, SPITTING OUT THE OLD AND TAKING IN THE NEW, IMITATING THE MOVEMENTS OF BEARS AND BIRDS...

THESE ARE JUST FOR LONGEVITY AND ARE WHAT PRACTITIONERS OF THE DOAYIN EXERCISES, HEALTH NUTS, AND PENG ZU ACOLYTES LIKE TO DO.

BUT THESE ARE ALL UNNATURAL AND CAN END UP BEING DETRIMENTAL.

IF YOU CAN BE SUPERIOR WITHOUT INTENTIONALLY CURBING AMBITION, PRACTICE SELF-CULTIVATION WITHOUT INTENTIONALLY BEING MORAL, GOVERN WITHOUT CONCERN FOR GREAT ACHIEVEMENTS OR REPUTATION, BE LEISURELY WITHOUT THE SEA OR RIVERS, ATTAIN LONGEVITY WITHOUT STRANGE EXERCISES, LOSE EVERYTHING AND YET POSSESS ALL THINGS, AND BE TRANQUIL WITHOUT GOING TO EXTREMES, THEN GOOD THINGS WILL FOLLOW. THIS IS THE DAO OF NATURE, THE VIRTUE OF THE SAGE.

PEOPLE NORMALLY RELY ON AMBITION, VIRTUES AND MORALITY, ACHIEVEMENT AND REPUTATION, THE SEA AND RIVERS, AND TRAINING AND DISCIPLINE AS THE BEST METHODS FOR SELF-CULTIVATION AND ESTABLISHING A CAREER, BUT TO ONE WHO UNDERSTANDS THE DAO, THEY ARE ALL SHACKLES AND CHAINS.

ENERGY AND SPIRIT

IF THE BODY TOILS WITHOUT REST, IT WILL BECOME FATIGUED...

IF ONE'S ENERGY IS USED WITHOUT A BREAK, IT WILL BE EXHAUSTED...

FOR INSTANCE, IT IS THE NATURE OF WATER TO BE CLEAR WHEN IT IS NOT MADE TURBID, TO BE CALM WHEN IT IS NOT STIRRED UP...

IF IT IS BLOCKED UP AND UNABLE TO FLOW, IT CANNOT BE CLEAR. THIS IS A NATURAL PHENOMENON.

SO IT IS SAID THAT CLARITY WITHOUT TURBIDITY, TRANQUILLITY WITHOUT ALTERATION, SIMPLICITY WITHOUT ACTION, AND MOVEMENT WITH THE NATURAL WAY ARE ALL THE DAO OF NURTURING THE SPIRIT.

THE SPIRIT IS LIKE A PRECIOUS SWORD. IT SHOULD BE KEPT IN A CASE AND NOT IMPRUDENTLY REMOVED.

COMMON PEOPLE EMPHASIZE SELFISH BENEFIT, UPRIGHT PEOPLE EMPHASIZE REPUTATION, CAPABLE PEOPLE PRAISE AMBITION, AND SAGES CHERISH THE SPIRIT!

CHAPTER 15
CURBING AMBITION

形勞而不休則弊，精用而不已則勞，勞則竭。水之性，不雜則清，莫動則平；鬱閉而不流，亦不能清；天德之象也。故曰：純粹而不雜，靜一而不變，淡而無為，動而以天行，此養神之道也。夫有干越之劍者，柙而藏之，不敢用也，寶之至也。精神四達並流，無所不極，上際於天，下蟠於地，化育萬物，不可為象，其名為同帝。

103

古之所謂隱士者，非伏其身而弗見也，非閉其言而不出也，非藏其知而不發也，時命大謬也。當時命而大行乎天下，則反一無跡；不當時命而大窮乎天下，則深根寧極而待：此存身之道也。

RECLUSES

RECLUSES OF OLD DIDN'T NECESSARILY HIDE THEMSELVES AWAY FROM THE WORLD.

THEY WERE MEN OF GREAT WISDOM, AND AT THE APPROPRIATE TIMES THEY WOULD COME OUT TO IMPLEMENT THE DAO THROUGHOUT THE LAND...

IF THE TIMES WERE NOT APPROPRIATE, THEY WOULD CONCEAL THEIR WISDOM, BECOME ONE WITH NATURE, AND DISAPPEAR FROM SIGHT.

IN THE PAST, PEOPLE WHO KNEW HOW TO TAKE CARE OF THEMSELVES DID NOT GO AROUND POINTING OUT THEIR OWN WISDOM; THEY DIDN'T USE THEIR TIMING AND INGENUITY TO BRING SUFFERING TO THE PEOPLE; AND THEY DIDN'T LET GREED TIE DOWN THEIR OWN VIRTUE.

CHAPTER 17

An Autumn Flood

秋水時至，百川灌河，涇流之大，兩涘渚崖之間，不辯牛馬。於是焉河伯欣然自喜，以天下之美為盡在己。

順流而東行，至於北海，東面而視，不見水端，於是焉河伯始旋其面目，望洋向若而歎曰：「聞道百，以為莫己若」者，我之謂也。

且夫我嘗聞少仲尼之聞而輕伯夷之義者，始吾弗信，今我睹子之難窮也，吾非至於子之門則殆矣，吾長見笑於大方之家。」

北海若曰：「井蛙不可以語於海者，拘於虛也；夏蟲不可以語於冰者，篤於時也；曲士不可以語於道者，束於教也。

今爾出於崖涘，觀於大海，乃知爾醜，爾將可以語於大理矣。

AN AUTUMN FLOOD

ONCE, WHEN THE AUTUMN RAINS FELL, ALL THE STREAMS AND TRIBUTARIES POURED INTO THE YELLOW RIVER. AS THE RIVER SWELLED, THE BANKS FLOODED AND ALL THE SANDBARS DISAPPEARED.

HA HA HA. I'M THE LARGEST BODY OF WATER IN THE LAND.

THE LORD OF THE YELLOW RIVER FLOWED ALONG, DELIGHTED WITH HIS AWESOME BEAUTY. THEN, HE FLOWED INTO THE NORTHERN SEA AND LOOKED IN EVERY DIRECTION. HE SAW A BODY OF WATER SO VAST THAT HE COULDN'T SEE THE OTHER SHORE...

WOW! *THIS* IS THE LARGEST BODY OF WATER!

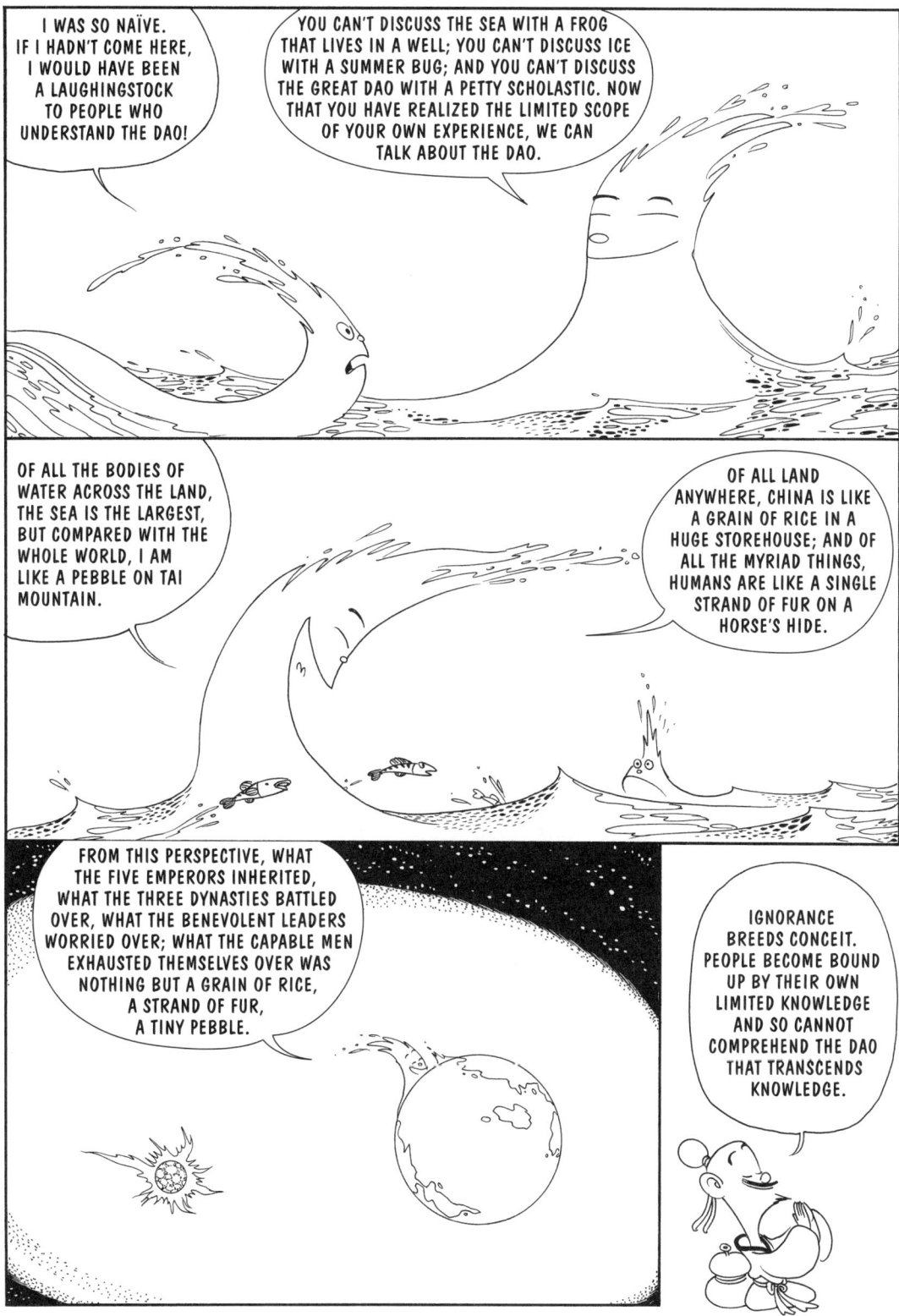

I WAS SO NAÏVE. IF I HADN'T COME HERE, I WOULD HAVE BEEN A LAUGHINGSTOCK TO PEOPLE WHO UNDERSTAND THE DAO!

YOU CAN'T DISCUSS THE SEA WITH A FROG THAT LIVES IN A WELL; YOU CAN'T DISCUSS ICE WITH A SUMMER BUG; AND YOU CAN'T DISCUSS THE GREAT DAO WITH A PETTY SCHOLASTIC. NOW THAT YOU HAVE REALIZED THE LIMITED SCOPE OF YOUR OWN EXPERIENCE, WE CAN TALK ABOUT THE DAO.

OF ALL THE BODIES OF WATER ACROSS THE LAND, THE SEA IS THE LARGEST, BUT COMPARED WITH THE WHOLE WORLD, I AM LIKE A PEBBLE ON TAI MOUNTAIN.

OF ALL LAND ANYWHERE, CHINA IS LIKE A GRAIN OF RICE IN A HUGE STOREHOUSE; AND OF ALL THE MYRIAD THINGS, HUMANS ARE LIKE A SINGLE STRAND OF FUR ON A HORSE'S HIDE.

FROM THIS PERSPECTIVE, WHAT THE FIVE EMPERORS INHERITED, WHAT THE THREE DYNASTIES BATTLED OVER, WHAT THE BENEVOLENT LEADERS WORRIED OVER; WHAT THE CAPABLE MEN EXHAUSTED THEMSELVES OVER WAS NOTHING BUT A GRAIN OF RICE, A STRAND OF FUR, A TINY PEBBLE.

IGNORANCE BREEDS CONCEIT. PEOPLE BECOME BOUND UP BY THEIR OWN LIMITED KNOWLEDGE AND SO CANNOT COMPREHEND THE DAO THAT TRANSCENDS KNOWLEDGE.

與語大理矣。天下之水，莫大於海，萬川歸之，不知何時止而不盈；尾閭泄之，不知何時已而不虛；……吾在天地之間，猶小石小木之在大山也，方存乎見少，又奚以自多！計四海之在天地之間也，不似礨空之在大澤乎？計中國之在海內，不似稀米之在大倉乎？號物之數謂之萬，人處一焉；人卒九州，穀食之所生，舟車之所通，人處一焉。此其比萬物也，不似豪末之在於馬體乎？五帝之所連，三王之所爭，仁人之憂，任士之所勞，盡此矣。伯夷辭之以為名，仲尼語之以為博，此其自多也，不似爾向之自多於水乎？」

河伯曰：「然則吾大天地而小豪末，可乎？」北海若曰：「否。夫物，量無窮，時無止，分無常，終始無故。是故大知觀於遠近，故小而不寡，大而不多，知量無窮；證曏今故，故遙而不悶，掇而不跂，知時無止；察乎盈虛，故得而不喜，失而不憂，知分之無常也；明乎坦塗，故生而不說，死而不禍，知終始之不可故也。計人之所知，不若其所不知；其生之時，不若未生之時；以其至小求窮其至大之域，是故迷亂而不能自得也。由此觀之，又何以知豪末之足以定至細之倪！又何以知天地之足以窮至大之域！」

河伯曰：「世之議者皆曰：『至精無形，至大不可圍。』是信情乎？」北海若曰：「夫自細視大者不盡，自大視細者不明。夫精，小之微也；垺，大之殷也；故異便。此勢之有也。夫精粗者，期於有形者也；無形者，數之所不能分也；不可圍者，數之所不能窮也。可以言論者，物之粗也；可以意致者，物之精也；言之所不能論，意之所不能察致者，不期精粗焉。」

109

河伯曰：「若物之外，若物之內，惡至而倪貴賤？惡至而倪小大？」北海若曰：「以道觀之，物無貴賤；以物觀之，自貴而相賤，貴賤不在己。以差觀之，因其所大而大之，則萬物莫不大；因其所小而小之，則萬物莫不小；知天地之為稊米也，知豪末之為丘山也，則差數等矣。以功觀之，因其所有而有之，則萬物莫不有；因其所無而無之，則萬物莫不無；知東西之相反而不可以相無，則功分定矣。」

STATUS
AND
THE
DAO

ARE THERE DIFFERENCES IN STATUS AMONG THE MYRIAD THINGS?

FROM THE STANDPOINT OF THE DAO, ALL OF THE MYRIAD THINGS ARE OF EQUAL STATUS. BUT FROM THE STANDPOINT OF EACH OF THE MYRIAD THINGS, EACH SEES ITSELF AS VALUABLE AND THE OTHERS AS BASE. FROM THE STANDPOINT OF SOCIAL CONVENTION, STATUS IS SOMETHING THAT OTHERS THRUST ON YOU, WITHOUT ANY SAY OF YOUR OWN.

WEALTHY.

VALUABLE.

POOR.

BASE.

A THING ITSELF DOES NOT POSSESS GOODNESS OR STATUS; RATHER, THOSE ARE ENTIRELY REFLECTIONS OF EXTERNAL VALUE JUDGMENTS. IF YOU CAN GET BEYOND CONVENTIONAL CONCEPTS OF STATUS, YOU CAN BE FREE OF ALL OBSTACLES.

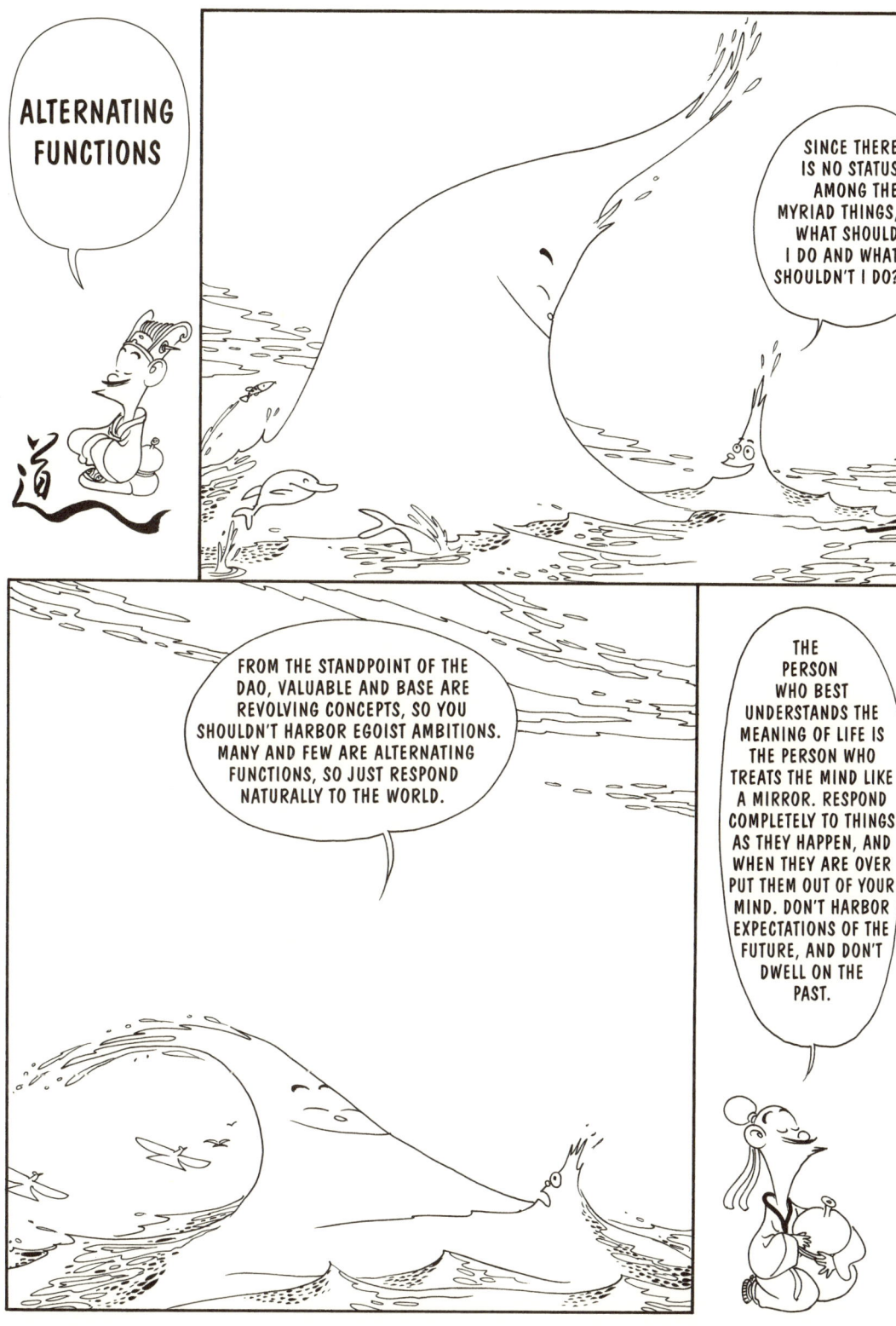

ALTERNATING FUNCTIONS

SINCE THERE IS NO STATUS AMONG THE MYRIAD THINGS, WHAT SHOULD I DO AND WHAT SHOULDN'T I DO?

FROM THE STANDPOINT OF THE DAO, VALUABLE AND BASE ARE REVOLVING CONCEPTS, SO YOU SHOULDN'T HARBOR EGOIST AMBITIONS. MANY AND FEW ARE ALTERNATING FUNCTIONS, SO JUST RESPOND NATURALLY TO THE WORLD.

THE PERSON WHO BEST UNDERSTANDS THE MEANING OF LIFE IS THE PERSON WHO TREATS THE MIND LIKE A MIRROR. RESPOND COMPLETELY TO THINGS AS THEY HAPPEN, AND WHEN THEY ARE OVER PUT THEM OUT OF YOUR MIND. DON'T HARBOR EXPECTATIONS OF THE FUTURE, AND DON'T DWELL ON THE PAST.

河伯曰：「然則我何為乎，何不為乎？吾辭受趣舍，吾終奈何？」北海若曰：「以道觀之，何貴何賤，是謂反衍，無拘而志，與道大蹇。何少何多，是謂謝施。」

河伯曰⋯「然則何貴於道邪?」北海若曰⋯「知道者必達於理,達於理者必明於權,明於權者不以物害己。

至德者,火弗能熱,水弗能溺,寒暑弗能害,禽獸弗能賊。非謂其薄之也,言察乎安危,寧於禍福,謹於去就,

莫之能害也。故曰⋯天在內,人在外,德在乎天。知天人之行,本乎天,位乎得;蹢躅而屈伸,反要而語極。」

FIRE DOESN'T BURN

WHAT'S THE VALUE, THEN, OF STUDYING THE DAO?

IF YOU UNDERSTAND THE DAO, YOU WILL UNDERSTAND HOW TO ADAPT TO CHANGES, AND YOU WILL BE FREE FROM DANGER.

FIRE WON'T BURN YOU AND WATER WON'T DROWN YOU. ONLY A PERSON OF THE DAO CAN ATTAIN THIS.

A PERSON OF THE DAO ADAPTS TO ALL CIRCUMSTANCES. IF SUFFERING, HE IMMERSES HIMSELF IN THE SUFFERING, AND IF JOYFUL, HE IMMERSES HIMSELF IN THE JOY. BECAUSE HE BECOMES ONE WITH HIS ENVIRONMENT, THE ENVIRONMENT DOESN'T AFFECT HIM.

CHAPTER 17
AN AUTUMN FLOOD

河伯曰：「何謂天，何謂人？」北海若曰：「牛馬四足，是謂天；落馬首，穿牛鼻，是謂人。故曰：無以人滅天，無以故滅命，無以得殉名。謹守而勿失，是謂反其真。」

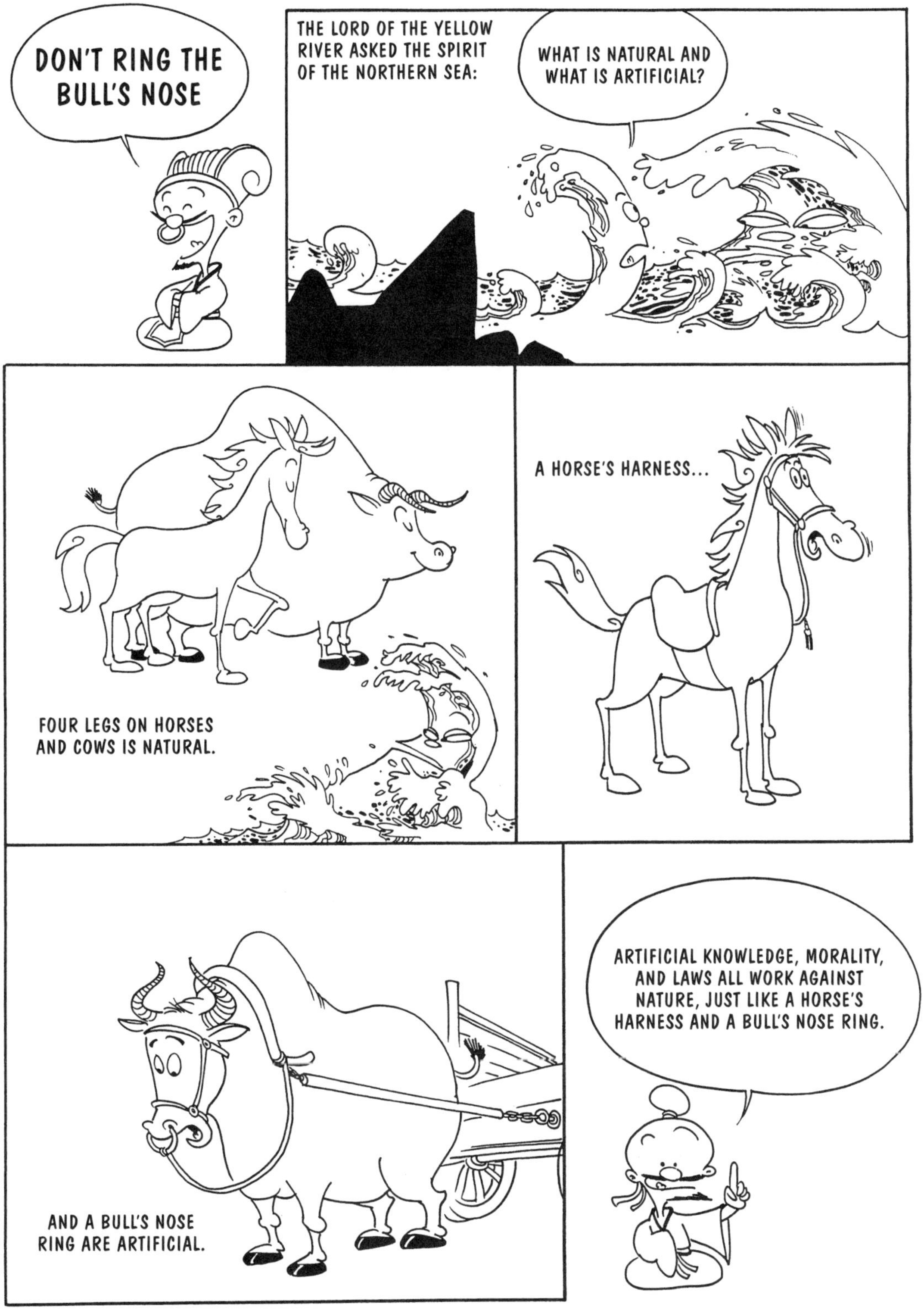
DON'T RING THE BULL'S NOSE
THE LORD OF THE YELLOW RIVER ASKED THE SPIRIT OF THE NORTHERN SEA:
WHAT IS NATURAL AND WHAT IS ARTIFICIAL?
FOUR LEGS ON HORSES AND COWS IS NATURAL.
A HORSE'S HARNESS...
AND A BULL'S NOSE RING ARE ARTIFICIAL.
ARTIFICIAL KNOWLEDGE, MORALITY, AND LAWS ALL WORK AGAINST NATURE, JUST LIKE A HORSE'S HARNESS AND A BULL'S NOSE RING.

夔謂蚿曰：「吾以一足趻踔而行，予無如矣。今子之使萬足，獨奈何？」蚿曰：「不然。子不見夫唾者乎？噴則大者如珠，小者如霧，雜而下者不可勝數也。今予動吾天機，而不知其所以然。」蚿謂蛇曰：「吾以眾足行，而不及子之無足，何也？」蛇曰：「夫天機之所動，何可易邪？吾安用足哉！」

THE WIND AND THE SNAKE

THE *KUI* IS A ONE-FOOTED CREATURE. THE MILLIPEDE HAS ONE THOUSAND FEET.

IT'S PERFECTLY CONVENIENT FOR ME TO WALK WITH JUST ONE FOOT. HOW DO YOU WALK WITH SO MANY?

IT'S MY NATURE TO WALK THIS WAY. IT'S NO PROBLEM AT ALL.

HOW COME YOU CAN MOVE FASTER WITH NO LEGS THAN I CAN WITH SO MANY?

I MOVE ACCORDING TO MY NATURAL MECHANISMS. WHAT DO I NEED LEGS FOR?

蛇謂風曰：「予動吾脊脅而行，則有似也。今子蓬蓬然起於北海，蓬蓬然入於南海，而似無有，何也？」風曰：「然。予蓬蓬然起於北海而入於南海也，然而指我則勝我，蹈我亦勝我。雖然，夫折大木，蜚大屋者，唯我能也，故以眾小不勝為大勝也。為大勝者，唯聖人能之。」

115

孔子遊於匡，宋人圍之數匝，而弦歌不惙，子路入見，曰：「何夫子之娛也？」孔子曰：「來！吾語女。我諱窮久矣，而不免，命也；求通久矣，而不得，時也。當堯、舜而天下無窮人，非知得也；當桀、紂而天下無通人，非知失也，時勢適然。夫水行不避蛟龍者，漁父之勇也；

COURAGE OF THE SAGE

ONE DAY WHILE JOURNEYING TO THE CITY OF KUANG WITH HIS STUDENTS, CONFUCIUS WAS SURROUNDED BY A SONG POSSE WHO MISTOOK HIM FOR THE CRIMINAL YANG HUO.

DON'T PANIC, JUST SIT STILL AND CONTINUE LISTENING TO ME TEACH.

BUT AREN'T YOU AFRAID, MASTER?

OF COURSE I AM, ZHONG YOU, BUT LISTEN...

NOT FEARING WATER DRAGONS IS THE COURAGE OF THE FISHERMAN.

NOT FEARING FEROCIOUS TIGERS IS THE COURAGE OF THE HUNTER.

HAVING NO FEAR ON THE BATTLEFIELD IS THE COURAGE OF THE WARRIOR.

COME ON!

TO UNDERSTAND THAT IN LIFE EVERYONE ENCOUNTERS BOTH SUCCESS AND FAILURE, AND THUS TO NOT BE AFRAID IN THE FACE OF ADVERSITY —THIS IS THE COURAGE OF THE SAGE.

AFTER A TIME, A LEADER CAME FORWARD TO APOLOGIZE, AND THE TROOPS DISPERSED.

I'M SORRY, WE THOUGHT YOU WERE YANG HUO.

EVERYONE MEETS WITH TIMES OF GOOD FORTUNE AND TIMES OF DISTRESS, AND IT IS IN TIMES OF DISTRESS THAT WE MUST USE OUR WISDOM TO OBSERVE AND WAIT PATIENTLY FOR A CHANGE FOR THE BETTER.

陸行不避兕虎者，獵夫之勇也；白刃交於前，視死若生者，烈士之勇也；知窮之有命，知通之有時，臨大難而不懼者，聖人之勇也。由處矣，吾命有所制矣。」無幾何，將甲者進，辭曰：「以為陽虎也，故圍之。今非也，請辭而退。」

117

蹴泥則沒足滅跗，

子獨不聞夫埳之鼃乎？謂東海之鱉曰：「吾樂與！吾跳梁乎井幹之上，入休乎缺甃之崖，赴水則接掖持頤，

還蚷蟹與科斗，莫吾能若也。且夫擅一壑之水，而跨跱埳井之樂，此亦至矣，夫子奚不時來入觀乎！」東海之鱉左足未入，而右膝已縶矣。

119

於是逡巡而卻，告之海曰：「夫千里之遠，不足以舉其大；千仞之高，不足以極其深。禹之時十年九潦，而水弗為加益；湯之時八年七旱，而崖不為加損。夫不為頃久推移，不以多少進退者，此亦東海之大樂也。」於是埳井之鼃聞之，適適然驚，規規然自失也。且夫知不知是非之竟，而猶欲觀於莊子之言，是猶使蚊負山，商蚷馳河也，必不勝任矣。且夫知不知論極妙之言而自適一時之利者，是非埳井之鼃與？

120

LEARNING HOW TO WALK IN HANDAN

THERE WAS ONCE A YOUNG MAN FROM YAN WHO WENT TO THE CITY OF HANDAN TO LEARN HOW TO WALK LIKE THE PEOPLE THERE.

BUT NOT ONLY DID HE NOT LEARN HOW TO WALK LIKE THEM, HE FORGOT HOW TO WALK ALTOGETHER!

AH! I CAN'T WALK!

SO HE HAD TO CRAWL HOME.

AT THE OUTSET, PEOPLE WHO STUDY ARE IN SEARCH OF THE ESSENCE OF NATURE, BUT AFTER A WHILE, THEY GET LOST IN THE FOREST OF BOOKS AND CAN'T GET OUT.

【子獨不聞夫壽陵餘子之學行於邯鄲與？未得國能，又失其故行矣，直匍匐而歸耳。

莊子釣於濮水，楚王使大夫二人往先焉，曰：「願以竟內累矣！」莊子持竿不顧，曰：「吾聞楚有神龜，死已三千歲矣，王巾笥而藏之廟堂之上。此龜者，寧其死為留骨而貴乎？寧其生而曳尾於塗中乎？」二大夫曰：「寧生而曳尾塗中。」莊子曰：「往矣！吾將曳尾於塗中。」

TAIL IN THE MUD

122

惠子相梁，莊子往見之。或謂惠子曰：「莊子來，欲代子相。」於是惠子恐，搜於國中三日三夜。莊子往見之，曰：「南方有鳥，其名鵷鶵，子知之乎？夫鵷鶵，發於南海而飛於北海，非梧桐不止，

非練實不食，非醴泉不飲。於是鴟得腐鼠，鵷鶵過之，仰而視之曰：『嚇！』今子欲以子之梁國而嚇我邪？」

AND EATS ONLY TENDER BAMBOO SHOOTS.

AND DRINKS ONLY FRESH SPRING WATER.

ONE DAY WHILE IN FLIGHT, THE *YUANCHU* SPOTTED A CROW LUNCHING ON A RAT.

CAW!

SEEING THE *YUANCHU*, THE CROW WAS AFRAID IT WOULD STEAL THE RAT, SO IT RAISED ITS HEAD AND SCREECHED WITH ALL ITS MIGHT.

ARE YOU GOING TO SCREECH AT ME?

HIGH POSITIONS MAY BE NECESSARY TO SOCIETY, BUT A WISE PERSON VIEWS THEM AS HE WOULD A CHEAP INN— NO REASON TO STICK AROUND.

莊子與惠子遊於濠梁之上。莊子曰：「儵魚出游從容，是魚樂也。」惠子曰：「子非魚，安知魚之樂？」莊子曰：「子非我，安知我不知魚之樂？」惠子曰：「我非子，固不知子矣；子固非魚也，子之不知魚之樂，全矣。」莊子曰：「請循其本，子曰『女安知魚樂』云者，既已知吾知之而問我，我知之濠上也。」

125

CHAPTER 18
Ultimate Joy

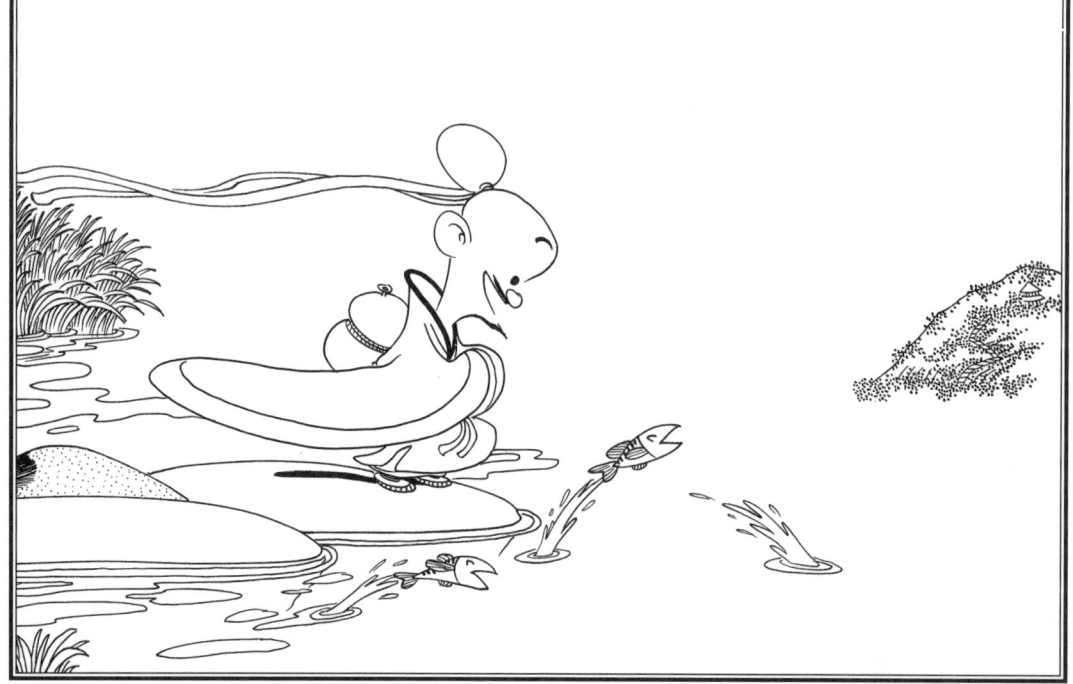

天下有至樂無有哉？有可以活身者無有哉？今奚為奚據？奚避奚處？奚就奚去？奚樂奚惡？夫天下之所尊者，富貴壽善也；所樂者，身安厚味美服好色音聲也；

ULTIMATE
JOY

IS THERE SUCH A THING AS ULTIMATE JOY? OR A WAY TO PRESERVE LIFE? THERE IS AN ANSWER.

BUT PEOPLE DON'T KNOW WHAT TO GRAB AHOLD OF AND WHAT TO LET GO! THEY DON'T KNOW WHAT TO DO OR RELY ON, WHAT TO AVOID OR WHAT TO ABIDE IN, WHAT TO ACCOMMODATE OR WHAT TO ELIMINATE, WHAT TO LIKE OR WHAT TO DISLIKE.

WHAT MOST PEOPLE RESPECT ARE WEALTH, PRESTIGE, LONGEVITY, AND SKILL.

WHAT THEY LIKE ARE PHYSICAL SECURITY, RICH FLAVORS, FINE CLOTHING, BRIGHT COLORS, AND GOOD MUSIC.

所下者，貧賤夭惡也；所苦者，身不得安逸，口不得厚味，形不得美服，目不得好色，耳不得音聲；若不得者，則大憂以懼。其為形也亦愚哉！

莊子妻死，惠子弔之，莊子則方箕踞鼓盆而歌。惠子曰：「與人居，長子老身，死不哭亦足矣，又鼓盆而歌，不亦甚乎！」莊子曰：「不然。是其始死也，我獨何能無概然！察其始而本無生，非徒無生也而本無形，非徒形也而本無氣。

ZHUANGZI DRUMS TO DEATH

WHEN ZHUANGZI'S WIFE DIED, HUIZI WENT TO PAY HIS RESPECTS. WHEN HE ARRIVED, HE SAW ZHUANGZI CROUCHED DOWN DRUMMING AND SINGING.

ALL THESE YEARS YOUR WIFE TAKES CARE OF THE HOUSE AND KIDS, THEN SHE GETS OLD AND DIES, AND NOT ONLY DO YOU NOT CRY, BUT YOU DRUM AND SING! THAT'S OUTRAGEOUS!

NOT REALLY. WHEN SHE HAD JUST PASSED AWAY, HOW COULD I NOT HAVE FELT ANYTHING?

BUT THEN I THOUGHT FOR A BIT: ORIGINALLY PEOPLE DON'T HAVE LIFE, OR EVEN A BODY OR SPIRIT...

雜乎芒芴之間，變而有氣，氣變而有形，形變而有生，今又變而之死，是相與為春秋冬夏四時行也。人且偃然寢於巨室，而我嗷嗷然隨而哭之，自以為不通乎命，故止也。」

支離叔與滑介叔觀於冥伯之丘，崑崙之虛，黃帝之所休。俄而柳生其左肘，其意蹶蹶然惡之。支離叔曰：「子惡之乎？」滑介叔曰：「亡，予何惡！生者，假借也；假之而生生者，塵垢也。死生為晝夜。且吾與子觀化而化及我，我又何惡焉！」

131

将子之春秋故及此乎？」於是語卒，援髑髏，枕而臥。夜半，髑髏見夢曰：「子之談者似辯士，

事，斧鉞之誅，而為此乎？將子有不善之行，愧遺父母妻子之醜，而為此乎？將子有凍餒之患，而為此乎？

莊子之楚，見空髑髏，髐然有形，撽以馬捶，因而問之，曰：「夫子貪生失理，而為此乎？將子有亡國之

ZHUANGZI DREAMS OF A SKELETON

ONE DAY ON HIS WAY TO CHU, ZHUANGZI HAPPENED UPON A HUMAN SKELETON.

DID YOU DIE BECAUSE YOU WERE GREEDY? OR WERE YOU HACKED TO PIECES WHEN YOUR COUNTRY WAS CONQUERED? OR DID YOU IMPLICATE YOUR PARENTS IN SOME HORRIBLE CRIME AND COMMIT SUICIDE OUT OF SHAME?

BONK!

DID YOU STARVE TO DEATH? DID YOU FREEZE TO DEATH? OR WERE YOU OLD AND JUST LAY DOWN HERE TO DIE?

NIGHT FELL, AND ZHUANGZI LAID HIMSELF DOWN TO SLEEP, USING THE SKULL AS HIS PILLOW.

ZZZ

FROM LISTENING TO YOU TODAY, YOU SOUND LIKE A SMOOTH TALKER.

視子所言，皆生人之累也，死則無此矣。子欲聞死之說乎？」莊子曰：「然。」髑髏曰：「死，無君於上，無臣於下；亦無四時之事，從然以天地為春秋，雖南面王樂，不能過也。」莊子不信，曰：「吾使司命復生子形，為子骨肉肌膚，反子父母妻子閭里知識，子欲之乎？」髑髏深矉蹙頞曰：「吾安能棄南面王樂，而復為人間之勞乎！」

CHAPTER 18
ULTIMATE JOY

昔者海鳥止於魯郊，魯侯御而觴之于廟，奏《九韶》以為樂，

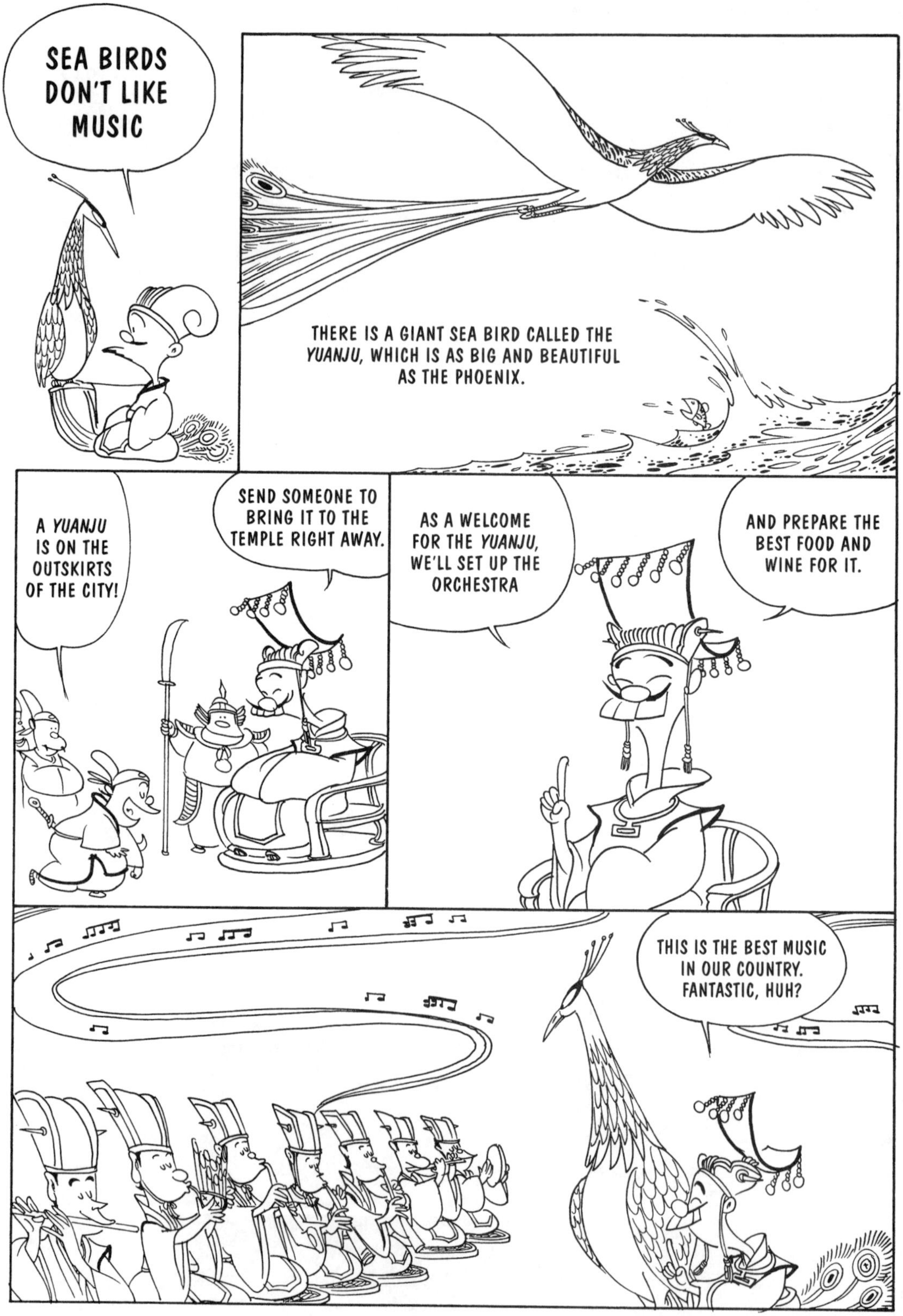
SEA BIRDS DON'T LIKE MUSIC
THERE IS A GIANT SEA BIRD CALLED THE *YUANJU*, WHICH IS AS BIG AND BEAUTIFUL AS THE PHOENIX.
A *YUANJU* IS ON THE OUTSKIRTS OF THE CITY!
SEND SOMEONE TO BRING IT TO THE TEMPLE RIGHT AWAY.
AS A WELCOME FOR THE *YUANJU*, WE'LL SET UP THE ORCHESTRA
AND PREPARE THE BEST FOOD AND WINE FOR IT.
THIS IS THE BEST MUSIC IN OUR COUNTRY. FANTASTIC, HUH?

具太牢以為膳。鳥乃眩視憂悲，不敢食一臠，不敢飲一杯，三日而死。此以己養養鳥也，非以鳥養養鳥也。故必相與異，其好惡故異也。……。

THIS IS ALL FOR YOU. GO AHEAD AND DIG IN.

THIS IS THE BEST WINE AROUND!

DRINK UP!

AFTER THREE DAYS OF NEITHER EATING NOR DRINKING, THE *YUANJU* UP AND DIED.

WHY DIDN'T YOU EAT? I GAVE YOU ALL OF THE BEST.

WHAT SOME PEOPLE BELIEVE TO BE THE BEST MUSIC AND THE BEST FOOD AREN'T NECESSARILY SO FOR EVERYONE. RAISE A BIRD ACCORDING TO A BIRD'S WANTS, NOT A PERSON'S. THE SAYING, "DO UNTO OTHERS AS YOU WOULD HAVE OTHERS DO UNTO YOU" IS NEVER REALLY APPLICABLE.

種有幾？……萬物皆出於機，皆入於機。

列子行食於道從，見百歲髑髏，攓蓬而指之曰：「唯予與女知而未嘗死，未嘗生也。若果養乎？予果歡乎？」

136

CHAPTER 19

Understanding Life

子列子問關尹曰：「至人潛行不窒，蹈火不熱，行乎萬物之上而不慄。請問何以至於此？」關尹曰：「是純氣之守也，非知巧果敢之列⋯⋯。則物之造乎不形而止乎無所化，夫得是而窮之者，物焉得而止焉！彼將處乎不淫之度，而藏乎無端之紀，遊乎萬物之所終始，壹其性，養其氣，合其德，以通乎物之所造。夫若是者，其天守全，其神無郤，物奚自入焉！

REALM OF THE PERFECT PERSON

A PERSON OF PERFECT VIRTUE IS QUITE REMARKABLE! WHEN A FOREST GOES UP IN FLAMES, HE DOESN'T FEEL HOT...

WHEN THE RIVERS FREEZE OVER, HE DOESN'T FEEL COLD...

WHEN LIGHTNING SHATTERS A MOUNTAINTOP OR WINDS ROIL THE SEA, HE ISN'T THE LEAST BIT AFRAID.

HE RIDES ON THE CLOUDS AND MOUNTS THE SUN AND MOON, TRAVELING BEYOND THE FOUR SEAS.

HE BECOMES ONE WITH THE TRANSFORMATIONS OF NATURE, AND SO THE TRANSFORMATIONS OF LIFE AND DEATH MEAN NOTHING TO HIM, LET ALONE HIS OWN PERSONAL BENEFIT OR HARM.

BECAUSE THERE IS NO ABSOLUTE RIGHT OR WRONG, HE ISN'T TIED DOWN BY EXTERNAL THINGS. BECAUSE HE FOLLOWS NATURE, TRANSCENDS THE MUNDANE WORLD, AND DOESN'T EVEN RECOGNIZE LIFE AND DEATH, WHY WOULD HE CARE ABOUT HIS OWN PERSONAL BENEFIT OR HARM?

夫醉者之墜車，雖疾不死。骨節與人同而犯害與人異，其神全也，乘亦不知也，墜亦不知也，死生驚懼不入乎其胸中，是故逆物而不慴。彼得全於酒而猶若是，而況得全於天乎？

139

仲尼適楚，出於林中，見痀僂者承蜩，猶掇之也。仲尼曰：「子巧乎！有道邪？」曰：「我有道也。五六月累丸二而不墜，則失者錙銖；

CATCHING CICADAS

ON HIS WAY TO CHU, CONFUCIUS PASSED THROUGH A FOREST, AND THERE HE SAW AN OLD MAN CATCHING CICADAS WITH A POLE, AS EASILY AS IF HE WERE GRABBING THEM WITH HIS HANDS...

EXCUSE ME, DO YOU CATCH THEM BY SKILL ALONE OR IS THERE A CERTAIN METHOD?

I HAVE A METHOD.

IN THE FIFTH AND SIX MONTHS, WHEN CICADAS ARE ABUNDANT, I PUT TWO BALLS ON THE TIP OF MY POLE, AND IF THEY DON'T FALL OFF, MY CHANCES OF MISSING A CICADA ARE QUITE SMALL.

FOR CATCHING CICADAS WITH A POLE, I HAVE A SET OF UNIQUE TRAINING METHODS...

THEN I PUT THREE BALLS ON THE TIP OF MY POLE, AND IF THEY DON'T FALL OFF, MY CHANCES OF MISSING A CICADA ARE ONE IN TEN.

THEN I DO FIVE BALLS, AND IF THEY DON'T FALL OFF, I CAN CATCH THE CICADAS AS IF I WERE USING MY BARE HAND.

WHEN I CATCH CICADAS, MY BODY IS AS STILL AS A TREE TRUNK, AND THE POLE IN MY HAND IS AS STEADY AS A THICK BRANCH...

AND DESPITE THE EXPANSIVENESS OF THE WORLD AND THE MULTITUDE OF THINGS IN IT, ALL I SEE ARE THE CICADA WINGS, AND NOTHING CAN DISTRACT ME FROM THEM. SO HOW CAN I MISS?

STUDENTS, PAY ATTENTION! AN UNDISTRACTED MIND BRINGS CONCENTRATION OF THE SPIRIT.

FOR AN EXPERT ARCHER, THERE IS NO BOW OR ARROW, NO SELF OR OTHER; ATTENTION IS CONCENTRATED ON THE TARGET AND THE SELF COALESCES WITH THE SURROUNDINGS; THE MYRIAD APPEARANCES ENTER THE MIND, BUT THE MIND TAKES NO HEED.

累三而不墜，則失者十一；累五而不墜，猶掇之也。吾處身也，若橛株拘；吾執臂也，若槁木之枝，雖天地之大，萬物之多，而唯蜩翼之知。吾不反不側，不以萬物易蜩之翼，何為而不得！」孔子顧謂弟子曰：「用志不分，乃凝於神，其痀僂丈人之謂乎！」

141

顔淵問仲尼曰：「吾嘗濟乎觴深之淵，津人操舟若神。吾問焉，曰：『操舟可學邪？』曰：『可。善游者數能。若乃夫沒人，則未嘗見舟而便操之也。』吾問焉而不吾告，敢問何謂也？」仲尼曰：「善游者數能，忘水也。

A SKIN-DIVER KNOWS HOW TO STEER A BOAT WITHOUT EVEN HAVING SEEN ONE BEFORE

BECAUSE TO HIM THE DEPTHS ARE LIKE HILLS AND A BOAT CAPSIZING IS NO WORSE THAN A CARRIAGE TIPPING OVER.

SINCE THE THOUGHT OF CAPSIZING DOESN'T BOTHER HIM, HE WOULD BE ABLE TO STEER WITH EASE AND CONFIDENCE!

IF BETTING WITH INEXPENSIVE TILES, AN ARCHER WOULD SHOOT WELL AND WITHOUT THE LEAST RESERVATION.

IF BETTING WITH PRECIOUS BELT HOOKS, HE WOULD FEEL A LITTLE UNSETTLED AND HIS ACCURACY WOULD REFLECT IT. AND IF BETTING WITH GOLD, THE BURDEN WOULD BE TOO MUCH, AND HE WOULD LOSE ALL ACCURACY.

A GOOD SWIMMER FORGETS THE WATER AND SO CAN COME AND GO WITH EASE. IF YOUR MIND BECOMES ATTACHED TO SOMETHING EXTERNAL YOU WILL LOSE YOUR CONCENTRATION AND YOUR SKILL. THAT'S WHY IT'S SAID THAT "THE ORDINARY MIND IS THE DAO."

THE SKILL-LEVEL OF THE ARCHER DOESN'T CHANGE, BUT AS SOON AS HE BEGINS TO CARE, HE IS PAYING ATTENTION TO SOMETHING EXTERNAL; AND WHENEVER YOU PAY ATTENTION TO SOMETHING EXTERNAL, YOU LOSE YOUR INTERNAL COMPOSURE.

若乃夫沒人之未嘗見舟而便操之也，彼視淵若陵，視舟之覆猶其車卻也。覆卻萬方陳乎前而不得入其舍，惡往而不暇！以瓦注者巧，以鈎注者憚，以黃金注者殙。其巧一也，而有所矜，則重外也。凡外重者內拙。」

祝宗人玄端以臨牢筴，說彘曰：「汝奚惡死？吾將三月豢汝，十日戒，三日齊，藉白茅，加汝肩尻乎彫俎之上，則汝為之乎？」為彘謀，曰：不如食以糠糟而錯之牢筴之中，自為謀，則苟生有軒冕之尊，死得於腞楯之上，聚僂之中則為之。為彘謀則去之，自為謀則取之，所異彘者何也？

THE SACRIFICIAL PIGS

ONE DAY THE MINISTER OF SACRIFICIAL CEREMONIES WENT TO THE PIGPEN IN HIS COURT ROBES AND SAID TO THE PIGS:

WHY SHOULD YOU GUYS FEAR DEATH? I GIVE YOU THE BEST FEED FOR THREE MONTHS, THEN PRACTICE AUSTERITIES FOR TEN DAY, AND FAST FOR THREE DAYS...

AND FINALLY, I PUT YOU ON A HOLY SACRIFICIAL PEDESTAL. THAT'S NOT ENOUGH GLORY FOR YOU?

AFTER A BIT, THE MINISTER BEGAN TO LOOK AT IT FROM THE PIGS' POINT OF VIEW...

I GUESS YOU'RE BETTER OFF EATING SLOP AND STAYING IN THE PEN!

IF A PERSON CAN THINK THIS WAY ON BEHALF OF A PIG, WHY WOULD HE STILL INSIST ON PURSUING GLORY AND STATUS AND MAKING HIMSELF THE SACRIFICIAL ANIMAL UP THERE ON THE PEDESTAL?

SWIMMING IN A WATERFALL

CONFUCIUS WENT TO SEE A WATERFALL OUTSIDE LÜLIANG. WATER RUSHED DOWN FROM 150 FEET UP, AND MIST BILLOWED OUT FOR NINE MILES.

AHH! A SUICIDE!

HURRY AND GO SAVE HIM!

YES, MASTER!

IT'S NOT A SUICIDE, HE'S JUST SWIMMING!

IS THERE SOME SPECIAL METHOD FOR SWIMMING IN RUSHING WATER?

NO, I DON'T HAVE ANY SPECIAL METHOD. I'VE BEEN AROUND WATER SO LONG THAT IT'S SECOND NATURE FOR ME. I GO IN WITH THE EDDIES AND OUT WITH THE SWELLS, FOLLOWING THE FLOW OF THE WATER INSTEAD OF MY OWN WILL.

CHAPTER 19
UNDERSTANDING LIFE

孔子觀於呂梁，縣水三十仞，流沫四十里，黿鼉魚鼈之所不能游也。見一丈夫游之，以為有苦而欲死也，使弟子並流而拯之。數百步而出，被髮行歌而游於塘下。孔子從而問焉，曰：「吾以子為鬼，察子則人也。請問，蹈水有道乎？」曰：「亡，吾無道。吾始乎故，長乎性，成乎命。與齊俱入，與汨偕出，從水之道而不為私焉。此吾所以蹈之也。」

145

梓慶削木為鐻，鐻成，見者驚猶鬼神。魯侯見而問焉，曰：「子何術以為焉？」對曰：「臣工人，何術之有！雖然，有一焉。臣將為鐻，未嘗敢以耗氣也，必齊以靜心。齊三日，而不敢懷慶賞爵祿；齊五日，不敢懷非譽巧拙；齊七日，輒然忘吾有四枝形體也。當是時也，無公朝，其巧專而外骨消；然後入山林，觀天性；形軀至矣，然後成見鐻，然後加手焉；不然則已。則以天合天，器之所以疑神者，其是與！」

QING BUILDS A BELL-STAND

THE WOODWORKER QING SPECIALIZED IN BELL-STANDS, AND ANYONE WHO SAW THEM WAS ASTOUNDED BY THEIR SUPERNATURAL WORKMANSHIP.

THAT'S FANTASTIC! WHAT'S YOUR TRICK?

WHEN I MAKE A BELL-STAND, I DON'T WANT TO EXHAUST MY ENERGIES, SO FIRST I FAST. AFTER FASTING FOR THREE DAYS, I HAVE DISMISSED ALL THOUGHT OF PAYMENT OR REWARD.

AFTER FIVE DAYS, I HAVE NO FEARS OF RUINING MY REPUTATION DUE TO POOR CRAFTSMANSHIP.

AFTER SEVEN DAYS, I HAVE DISMISSED ALL AWARENESS OF MY OWN BODY.

AT THIS POINT, I GO INTO THE FOREST AND OBSERVE THE NATURAL SHAPES OF THE TREES.

IF I FIND JUST THE RIGHT SHAPES, I FIT THEM TOGETHER AS BELL-STANDS AND TOUCH THEM UP BY HAND. IF I CAN'T FIND THEM, THEN I DON'T MAKE THE BELL-STAND. THIS IS WHY THEY SEEM SUPERNATURAL.

THE WOODWORKER QING WORKED IN ACCORDANCE WITH NATURE, SO HIS BELL-STANDS LOOKED LIKE THEY WERE SHAPED NATURALLY, WITHOUT A TRACE OF ARTIFICE.

DONGYE JI HAS AN ACCIDENT

DONGYE JI WAS A FAMOUSLY SKILLED CHARIOTEER, AND ONE TIME WHEN HE WAS WORKING WITH DUKE ZHUANG'S HORSES, HE RAN THE HORSES A HUNDRED TIMES AROUND THE TRACK.

YAN HE SAW THIS AND WENT TO THE DUKE:

SOMETHING'S GOING TO HAPPEN TO DONGYE'S HORSES.

REALLY?

DONGYE JI JUST HAD AN ACCIDENT.

HOW DID YOU KNOW SOMETHING WOULD HAPPEN?

THE HORSES' ENERGY WAS ALREADY DEPLETED, AND HE WAS STILL PUSHING THEM. SO I KNEW SOMETHING BAD WAS BOUND TO HAPPEN.

STRIVING HARD FOR SOMETHING EXHAUSTS YOUR ENERGY WITHOUT YOU REALIZING IT AND INEVITABLY RESULTS IN DISASTER.

東野稷以御見莊公，進退中繩，左右旋中規。莊公以為文弗過也，使之鉤百而反。顏闔遇之，入見曰：「稷之馬將敗。」公密而不應。少焉，果敗而反。公曰：「子何以知之？」曰：「其馬力竭矣，而猶求焉，故曰敗。」

心之適也；不內變，不外從，事會之適也。始乎適而未嘗不適者，忘適之適也。

工倕旋而蓋規矩，指與物化而不以心稽，故其靈臺一而不桎。忘足，履之適也；忘要，帶之適也；知忘是非，

THE CRAFTSMAN'S FINGERS

THE FINGERS OF CHUI THE CRAFTSMAN BECAME ONE WITH HIS TOOLS, ALLOWING HIM TO MAKE PERFECT LINES EFFORTLESSLY.

THE SHOES OF A PERSON WHO FORGETS HIS FEET ARE NATURALLY COMFORTABLE.

THE BELT OF A PERSON WHO FORGETS HIS WAIST IS NATURALLY COMFORTABLE.

THE MIND OF A PERSON WHO FORGETS RIGHT AND WRONG IS NATURALLY COMFORTABLE.

THE MOST COMFORTABLE OF ALL IS THE PERSON WHO FORGETS COMFORT ALTOGETHER.

DON'T FORCE YOUR MIND TO CONCENTRATE, AND DON'T FORCE YOURSELF TO BE IN HARMONY WITH THE EXTERNAL WORLD. JUST LET IT HAPPEN NATURALLY.

CHAPTER 20
Mountain Trees

莊子行於山中，見大木，枝葉盛茂，伐木者止其旁而不取也。問其故，曰：「此木以不材得終其天年。」夫子出於山，舍於故人之家。故人喜，命豎子殺鴈而烹之。豎子請曰：「其一能鳴，其一不能鳴，請奚殺？」主人曰：「殺不能鳴者。」明日，弟子問於莊子曰：「昨日山中之木，以不材得終其天年；今主人之鴈，以不材死；先生將何處？」

USELESS TREE...

USELESS GOOSE...

THOSE GIANT TREES ON THE MOUNTAIN YESTERDAY WERE ABLE TO LIVE FOR SO LONG BECAUSE THEY WERE USELESS. BUT THAT USELESS GOOSE WAS KILLED BECAUSE IT WAS USELESS. JUST HOW ARE WE SUPPOSED TO ACT?

THE ONLY WAY TO GET OUT OF THIS QUANDARY IS TO RIDE ALONG WITH THE DAO OF NATURE.

I TRY TO LIVE BETWEEN USEFULNESS AND USELESSNESS ... BUT EVEN SO, TROUBLE IS UNAVOIDABLE.

SO YOU JUST HAVE TO ADJUST TO THE CHANGES, REGARDLESS OF WHAT'S USEFUL AND WHAT'S USELESS.

USEFUL AND USELESS ARE RELATIVE, AND IT IS THE WISE PERSON WHO CAN TRANSCEND THEM.

HE'S USEFUL!

HE'S USELESS!

莊子笑曰：「周將處夫材與不材之間。材與不材之間，似之而非也，故未免乎累。若夫乘道德而浮遊則不然。」

孔子圍於陳蔡之間，七日不火食。太公任往弔之曰：「子幾死乎？」曰：「然。」「子惡死乎？」曰：「然。」

任曰：「予嘗言不死之道。東海有鳥焉，其名曰意怠。其為鳥也，翂翂翐翐，而似無能，引援而飛，迫脅而棲，

進不敢為前，

THE SWEET WATER IS GONE FIRST

#

CONFUCIUS WAS TOURING THE LAND ADVISING STATE LEADERS, WHEN HE AND HIS DISCIPLES SUDDENLY FOUND THEMSELVES TRAPPED BY WARRING ARMIES BETWEEN THE STATES OF CHEN AND CAI. IN THE ENSUING DAYS, CONFUCIUS AND HIS DISCIPLES RAN OUT OF FOOD AND DIDN'T EAT FOR A TOTAL OF SEVEN DAYS.

AFTER IT WAS OVER, AN OLD MAN NAMED REN APPROACHED CONFUCIUS.

IT LOOKS LIKE SOMEONE ALMOST GOT HURT THIS TIME.

YES ...

DIDN'T I TELL YOU HOW TO AVOID DANGER? THERE'S A BIRD NEAR THE EASTERN SEA CALLED THE LACKADAISICAL. AT FIRST GLANCE, THIS LACKADAISICAL DOESN'T SEEM TO BE VERY TALENTED. IN FLIGHT, IT INSISTS THAT OTHERS LEAD...

退不敢為後，食不敢先嘗，必取其緒。是故其行列不斥，而外人卒不得害，是以免於患。直木先伐，甘井先竭。子其意者飾知以驚愚，脩身以明汙，昭昭乎如揭日月而行，故不免也⋯⋯。」孔子曰：「善哉！」辭其交遊，去其弟子，逃於大澤；衣裘褐，食杼栗；入獸不亂群，入鳥不亂行。鳥獸不惡，而況人乎！

WHEN RESTING, IT HUDDLES IN THE MIDDLE OF THE FLOCK...

AND WHEN FEEDING, IT DOESN'T COMPETE FOR FOOD. THEREFORE, NOBODY EVER TRIES TO HURT IT.

STRAIGHT TREES GET CUT DOWN FIRST,

AND IT'S THE SWEET SPRING WATER THAT IS DRUNK FIRST.

CONFUCIUS WAS MUCH ENLIGHTENED BY THIS AND SUBSEQUENTLY TOOK LEAVE OF HIS FRIENDS AND DISCIPLES TO LIVE ALONE IN THE FOREST AND STUDY THE DAO.

YOU SEEM TO BE USING THE BRIGHTNESS OF YOUR WISDOM TO SHOW UP OTHER PEOPLE'S FAULTS. OF COURSE PEOPLE WON'T ACCEPT YOU FOR IT!

DON'T SHOW OFF YOUR WISDOM, OR OTHERS WILL FEAR AND RESENT YOU FOR IT.

子獨不聞假人之亡與？林回棄千金之璧，負赤子而趨。或曰：「為其布與？赤子之布寡矣；為其累與？赤子之累多矣；棄千金之璧，負赤子而趨，何也？」林回曰：「彼以利合，此以天屬也。」夫以利合者，迫窮禍患害相棄也；以天屬者，迫窮禍患害相收也。夫相收之與相棄亦遠矣。

154

莊子衣大布而補之，正廩係履而過魏王。魏王曰：「何先生之憊邪？」莊子曰：「貧也，非憊也。士有道

德不能行，憊也；衣弊履穿，貧也，非憊也；此所謂非遭時也。王獨不見夫騰猿乎？其得柟梓豫章也，攬

蔓其枝而王長其間，雖羿、蓬蒙不能眄睨也。及其得柘棘枳枸之間也，危行側視，振動悼慄，此筋骨非有

加急而不柔也，處勢不便，未足以逞其能也。

今處昏上亂相之間，而欲無憊，奚可得邪？此比干之見剖心

徵也夫！」

155

仲尼曰：「始用四達，爵祿並至而不窮，物之所利，乃非己也，吾命有在外者也。君子不為盜，賢人不為竊。吾若取之，何哉！故曰：鳥莫知於鷾鴯，目之所不宜處，不給視，雖落其實，棄之而走。其畏人也，而襲諸人閒，社稷存焉爾。」

SWALLOWS NEST IN THE EAVES

THE SWALLOW IS A WISE BIRD. WHEN IT SEES A PLACE IT SHOULDN'T GO, IT DOESN'T GO THERE,

AND WHEN IT DROPS A SEED FROM ITS MOUTH IN FLIGHT, IT DOESN'T STOP TO PICK IT UP.

THE SWALLOW HAS ALWAYS BEEN AFRAID AROUND PEOPLE, AND YET IT DARES TO BUILD ITS NESTS IN THE EAVES OF PEOPLE'S HOUSES.

THIS IS THE WISDOM OF HOW TO CONDUCT ONESELF IN LIFE.

MOST BIRDS FEAR PEOPLE AND BUILD THEIR NESTS IN THE MOUNTAINS OR HIGH UP IN TREES TO AVOID HARM. BUT SWALLOWS ARE SPECIAL—THEY LIVE CAREFREE IN THE VERY MIDST OF THE ONES THEY FEAR. THINK ABOUT HOW THE SWALLOW AVOIDS HARM.

THE MANTIS GETTING THE CICADA

MASTER, WHY THE SAD LOOK?

PEOPLE ARE ALWAYS FORGETTING THE DANGERS INVOLVED IN AMBITIOUS ENDEAVORS.

YESTERDAY, WHILE I WAS STROLLING THROUGH A CHESTNUT ORCHARD...

BONK!

I'LL GET YOU!

JUST THEN, I SAW A CICADA CHIRPING AWAY IN A TREE, THINKING IT WAS PERFECTLY SAFE...

莊周遊乎雕陵之樊，一異鵲自南方來者，翼廣七尺，目大運寸，感周之顙而集於栗林。莊周曰：「此何鳥哉，翼殷不逝，目大不覩？」蹇裳躩步，執彈而留之。一蟬，方得美蔭而忘其身，

螳蜋執翳而搏之，見得而忘其形；異鵲從而利之，見利而忘其真。莊周怵然曰：「噫！物固相累，二類相召也！」捐彈而反走，虞人逐而誶之。

莊周反入，三月不庭。藺且從而問之：「夫子何為頃間甚不庭乎？」莊周曰：「吾守形而忘身，觀於濁水而迷於清淵。……今吾遊於雕陵而忘吾身，異鵲感吾顙，遊於栗林而忘真，栗林虞人以吾為戮，吾所以不庭也。」

...NOT KNOWING THAT RIGHT BEHIND IT WAS A MANTIS ABOUT TO POUNCE.

HEE HEE...

AND WHILE THE MANTIS WAS CONCENTRATING ON GETTING THE CICADA, IT DIDN'T NOTICE THE BIRD GETTING READY TO GOBBLE IT UP.

WHAT DO YOU THINK YOU'RE DOING?

...

WHILE I WAS TRYING TO GET THE BIRD, I FORGOT THE DANGER I MYSELF WAS IN AND WAS ACCUSED OF STEALING CHESTNUTS. HOW EMBARRASSING.

WHEN PURSUING AN AMBITION, IT IS EASY TO SET OUR SIGHTS FORWARD, FORGETTING THE DANGER LURKING BEHIND.

CHAPTER 21

Tian Zifang

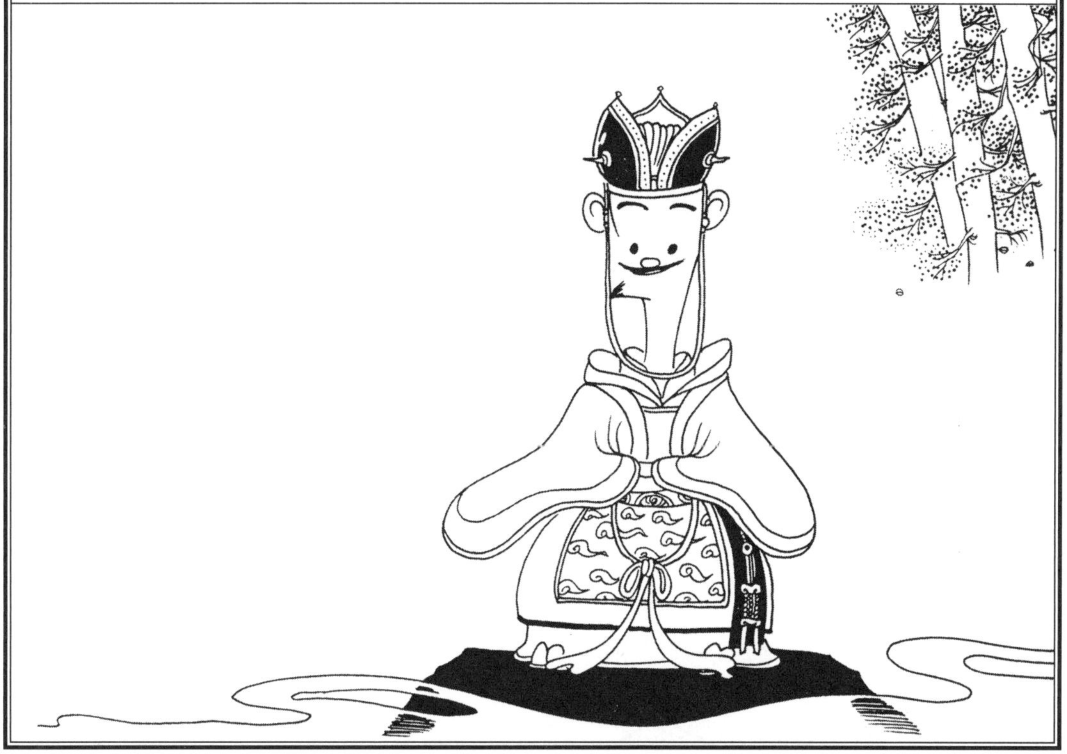

此服者，其罪死！』」

何謂少乎？」莊子曰：「周聞之，儒者冠圜冠者，知天時；履句屨者，知地形；緩佩玦者，事至而斷。君子有其道者，未必為其服也；為其服者，未必知其道也。公固以為不然，何不號於國中曰：『無此道而為

莊子見魯哀公，哀公曰：「魯多儒士，少為先生方者。」莊子曰：「魯少儒。」哀公曰：「舉魯國而儒服，

ONLY ONE CONFUCIAN IN LU

WHEN ZHUANGZI HAD AN AUDIENCE WITH DUKE AI OF LU, THE DUKE SAID:

HERE IN LU, MOST PEOPLE ARE CONFUCIAN. VERY FEW FOLLOW YOUR PATH!

ACTUALLY, THERE ARE VERY FEW CONFUCIANS IN LU!

HAVEN'T YOU SEEN EVERYONE IN CONFUCIAN CLOTHES? WHY DO YOU SAY THERE ARE VERY FEW?

I HAVE HEARD THAT THE ROUND CAP OF THE CONFUCIAN REPRESENTS HIS KNOWLEDGE OF ASTRONOMY, HIS RECTANGULAR SHOES REPRESENT HIS KNOWLEDGE OF GEOGRAPHY, AND HIS JADE BELT ORNAMENTS REPRESENT HIS DECISIVENESS.

ASTRONOMY

DECISIVENESS

GEOGRAPHY

A GENTLEMAN OF GOOD CULTIVATION DOESN'T NECESSARILY NEED TO WEAR THIS KIND OF COSTUME, AND A MAN WHO WEARS THIS KIND OF COSTUME ISN'T NECESSARILY A GENTLEMAN OF GOOD CULTIVATION.

I SUGGEST THAT YOU MAKE AN EDICT SAYING THAT ALL THOSE WHO AREN'T WELL-VERSED IN CONFUCIANISM AND YET WEAR CONFUCIAN-STYLE CLOTHES WILL BE PUT TO DEATH. THEN WE'LL SEE HOW MANY REAL CONFUCIANS THERE ARE.

OKAY!

於是哀公號之五日，而魯國無敢儒服者，獨有一丈夫，儒服而立乎公門。公即召而問以國事，千轉萬變而不窮。

莊子曰：「以魯國而儒者一人耳，可謂多乎？」

ISSUE AN EDICT: ALL THOSE WHO ARE NOT STRICT AND LEARNED CONFUCIANS AND YET WEAR THE CONFUCIAN COSTUME SHALL SUFFER A PENALTY OF DEATH!

AHH!

UH-OH.

EDICT
THE CONFUCIAN COSTUME MAY BE WORN ONLY BY TRUE CONFUCIANS. IMPOSTORS WILL BE EXECUTED!

I BETTER GO CHANGE

AFTER FIVE DAYS, ONLY ONE PERSON IN ALL OF LU DARED TO WEAR CONFUCIAN CLOTHING, AND HE CAME AND STOOD FACING THE PALACE.

THE DUKE CALLED HIM IN FOR QUESTIONING, AND SURE ENOUGH, HE WAS WELL-READ AND HAD ORTHODOX CONFUCIAN ANSWERS FOR EVERYTHING.

SEE, ONLY ONE CONFUCIAN IN ALL OF LU. WOULD YOU SAY THAT'S A LOT?

THE MOST IMPORTANT THING IN LIFE IS TO BE GENUINE, BUT PEOPLE OFTEN PUT ON FALSE APPEARANCES TO FULFILL OTHER PEOPLE'S EXPECTATIONS. THIS ISN'T GENUINENESS!

百里奚爵祿不入於心，故飯牛而牛肥，使秦穆公忘其賤，與之政也。有虞氏死生不入於心，故足以動人。

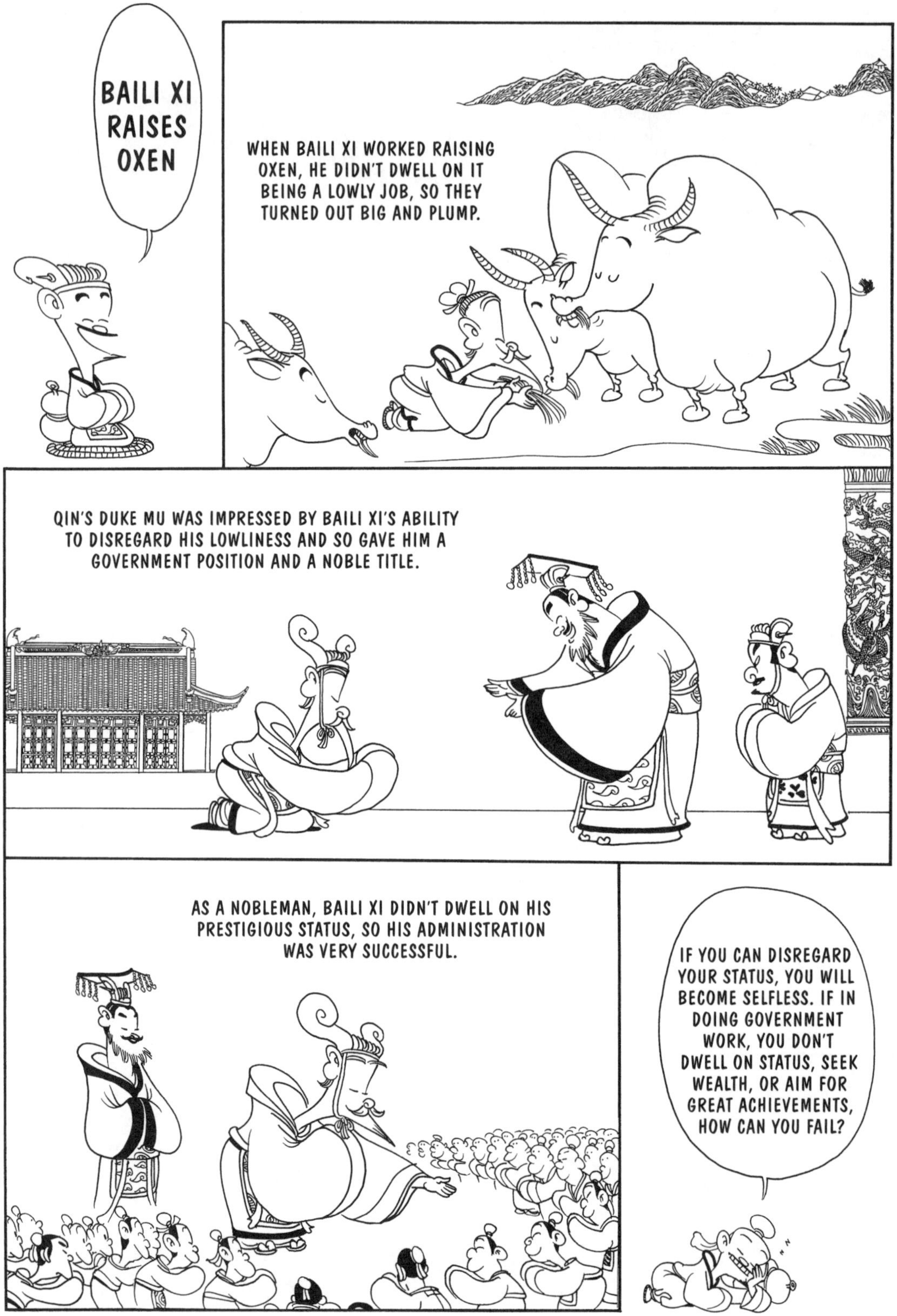
BAILI XI RAISES OXEN
WHEN BAILI XI WORKED RAISING OXEN, HE DIDN'T DWELL ON IT BEING A LOWLY JOB, SO THEY TURNED OUT BIG AND PLUMP.
QIN'S DUKE MU WAS IMPRESSED BY BAILI XI'S ABILITY TO DISREGARD HIS LOWLINESS AND SO GAVE HIM A GOVERNMENT POSITION AND A NOBLE TITLE.
AS A NOBLEMAN, BAILI XI DIDN'T DWELL ON HIS PRESTIGIOUS STATUS, SO HIS ADMINISTRATION WAS VERY SUCCESSFUL.
IF YOU CAN DISREGARD YOUR STATUS, YOU WILL BECOME SELFLESS. IF IN DOING GOVERNMENT WORK, YOU DON'T DWELL ON STATUS, SEEK WEALTH, OR AIM FOR GREAT ACHIEVEMENTS, HOW CAN YOU FAIL?

宋元君將畫圖，眾史皆至，受揖而立；舐筆和墨，在外者半。有一史後至者，儃儃然不趨，受揖不立，因之舍。

公使人視之，則解衣槃礴臝。君曰：「可矣，是真畫者也。」

列御寇為伯昏無人射，引之盈貫，措杯水其肘上，發之，適矢復沓，方矢復寓。當是時，猶象人也。伯昏無人曰：

「是射之射，非不射之射也。嘗與汝登高山，履危石，臨百仞之淵，若能射乎？」

PERFECT ARCHERY

LIEZI DEMONSTRATED HIS ARCHERY FOR BOHUN WUREN. HE SET A CUP OF WATER ON HIS ARM, AND FIRED ARROW AFTER ARROW WITH ALARMING SPEED.

WHEN THE FIRST ARROW HAD BEEN RELEASED, THE NEXT ARROW WAS ALREADY IN THE BOW; YET HE WAS AS STILL AS A STAKE AND NOT A DROP OF WATER SPILLED OUT OF THE CUP.

YOUR ARCHERY IS GOOD, BUT IT IS STILL INTENTIONAL. YOU'VE YET TO ATTAIN AN UNINTENTIONAL SKILL.

COME WITH ME!

於是無人遂登高山，履危石，臨百仞之淵，背逡巡，足二分垂在外，揖御寇而進之。御寇伏地，汗流至踵。

伯昏無人曰：「夫至人者，上闚青天，下潛黃泉，揮斥八極，神氣不變。今汝怵然有恂目之志，爾於中也殆矣夫！」

WHOA!

CAN YOU STAND STEADY AND SHOOT NOW?

AHH! I CAN'T DO IT! I CAN'T SHOOT HERE!

WHETHER ASCENDING TO THE BLUE SKY OR DESCENDING TO THE YELLOW SPRINGS, THE PERFECT PERSON'S COMPOSURE NEVER FALTERS. LOOK AT YOU, FRIGHTENED OUT OF YOUR WITS UP HERE. I'M AFRAID YOU'RE STILL A LONG WAY FROM THE DAO!

SOMEONE WHO SHOOTS AN ARROW WITH INTENTION RELIES ON SKILL, SOMEONE WHO SHOOTS WITHOUT INTENTION FLOWS WITH THE DAO. THE HIGHEST LEVEL OF ARCHERY IS FORGETTING THE SELF, FORGETTING THE ARROW, AND BECOMING ONE WITH THE DAO.

肩吾問於孫叔敖曰：「子三為令尹而不榮華，三去之而無憂色。吾始也疑子，今視子之鼻間栩栩然，子之用心獨奈何？」孫叔敖曰：「吾何以過人哉！吾以其來不可卻也，其去不可止也，吾以為得失之非我也，而無憂色而已矣。我何以過人哉！且不知其在彼乎，其在我乎？其在彼邪？亡乎我；在我邪？亡乎彼。方將躊躇，方將四顧，何暇至乎人貴人賤哉！」

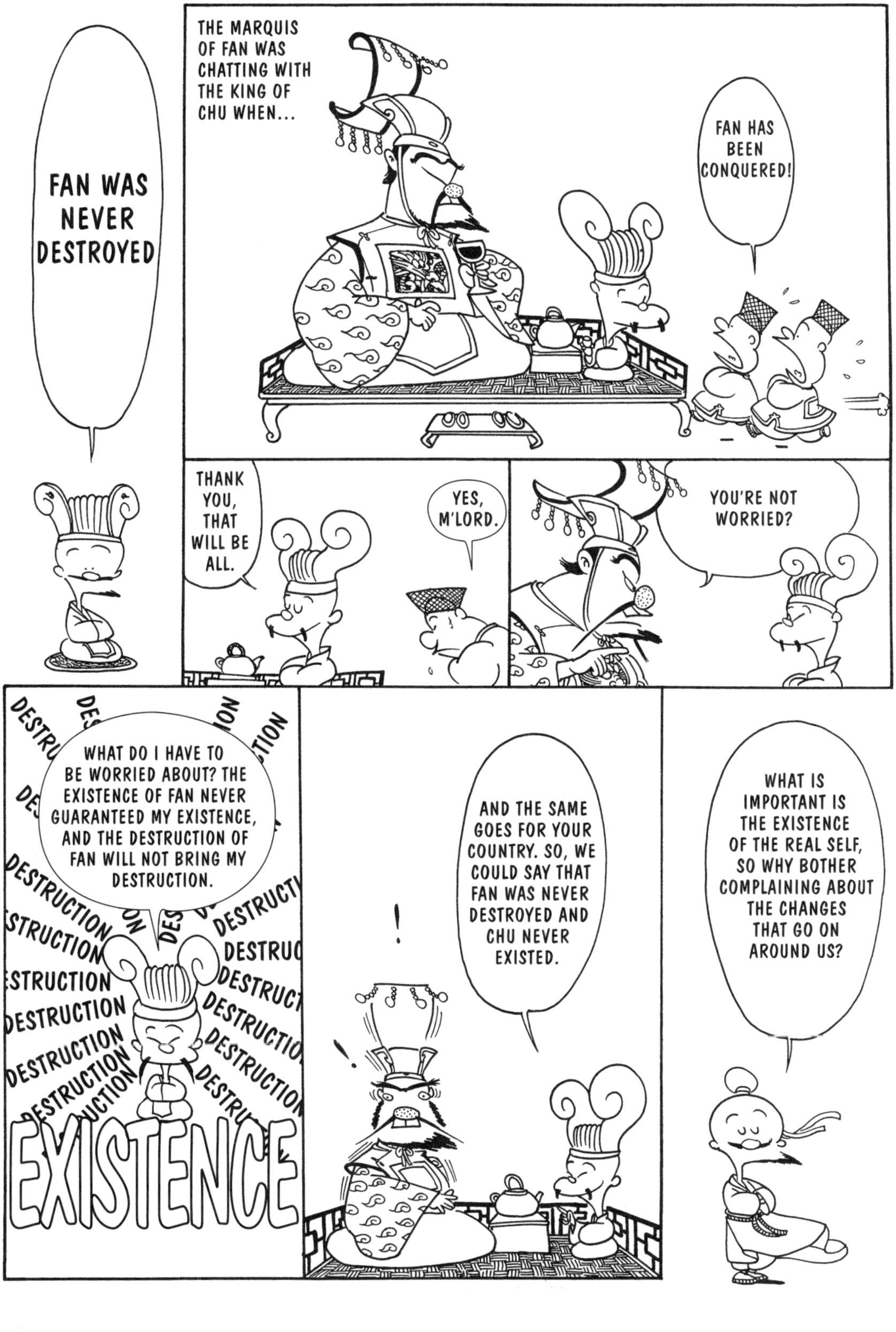
FAN WAS NEVER DESTROYED
THE MARQUIS OF FAN WAS CHATTING WITH THE KING OF CHU WHEN...
FAN HAS BEEN CONQUERED!
THANK YOU, THAT WILL BE ALL.
YES, M'LORD.
YOU'RE NOT WORRIED?
WHAT DO I HAVE TO BE WORRIED ABOUT? THE EXISTENCE OF FAN NEVER GUARANTEED MY EXISTENCE, AND THE DESTRUCTION OF FAN WILL NOT BRING MY DESTRUCTION.
DESTRUCTION
EXISTENCE
!
AND THE SAME GOES FOR YOUR COUNTRY. SO, WE COULD SAY THAT FAN WAS NEVER DESTROYED AND CHU NEVER EXISTED.
WHAT IS IMPORTANT IS THE EXISTENCE OF THE REAL SELF, SO WHY BOTHER COMPLAINING ABOUT THE CHANGES THAT GO ON AROUND US?

CHAPTER 21
TIAN ZIFANG

楚王與凡君坐，少焉，楚王左右曰凡亡者三。凡君曰：「凡之亡也，不足以喪吾存。夫『凡之亡也不足以喪吾存』，則楚之存不足以存存。由是觀之，則凡未始亡，而楚未始存也。」

CHAPTER 22

Knowledge Travels North

KNOWLEDGE AND THE DAO

ONE DAY, A MAN NAMED KNOWLEDGE WAS ON HIS WAY TO THE NORTH WHEN HE RAN INTO A FELLOW NAMED CAN'T SAY.

EXCUSE ME, COULD YOU TELL ME HOW TO THINK IN ORDER TO UNDERSTAND THE DAO, HOW TO ACT IN ORDER TO LIVE AT PEACE IN THE DAO, AND HOW TO ATTAIN THE DAO?

I CAN'T SAY!

I CAN'T SAY!

I CAN'T SAY!

? ?

NOT GETTING AN ANSWER, KNOWLEDGE CONTINUED ON TO THE SOUTH SIDE OF THE WHITE RIVER

WHERE HE RAN INTO ABSURD.

PARDON ME, I'D LIKE TO ASK YOU A FEW QUESTIONS.

NAMELY, HOW TO UNDERSTAND THE DAO, HOW TO LIVE AT PEACE IN THE DAO, AND HOW TO ATTAIN THE DAO?

知北遊於玄水之上，登隱弅之丘，而適遭無為謂焉。知謂無為謂曰：「予欲有問乎若：何思何慮則知道？何處何服則安道？何從何道則得道？」三問而無為謂不答也，非不答，不知答也。知不得問，反於白水之南，登狐闋之上，而睹狂屈焉。知以之言也問乎狂屈。

169

狂屈曰：「唉！予知之，將語若。」中欲言而忘其所欲言。知不得問，反於帝宮，見黃帝而問焉。黃帝曰：「無思無慮始知道，無處無服始安道，無從無道始得道。」知問黃帝曰：「我與若知之，彼與彼不知也，其孰是邪？」黃帝曰：「彼無為謂真是也，狂屈似之，我與汝終不近也。」

I KNOW ... AND I'D LIKE TO TELL YOU ... BUT, DARN IT, I FORGOT WHAT I WAS GOING TO SAY.

!

DON'T CONSCIOUSLY THINK, AND YOU'LL UNDERSTAND THE DAO. DON'T CONSCIOUSLY ACT, AND YOU'LL LIVE AT PEACE IN THE DAO. DON'T CONSCIOUSLY TRY, AND YOU'LL ATTAIN THE DAO.

??

STILL UNABLE TO GET AN ANSWER, KNOWLEDGE WENT TO SEE THE YELLOW EMPEROR.

OKAY, NOW YOU AND I KNOW THIS, BUT WHY IS IT THAT CAN'T SAY AND ABSURD DON'T KNOW?

OH! THERE YOU ARE MISTAKEN. THEY DO KNOW! CAN'T SAY IS ONE WITH THE DAO, AND ABSURD ISN'T FAR AWAY. IT IS YOU AND I WHO STILL HAVE A LONG WAY TO GO.

THE MAN NAMED KNOWLEDGE WAS OF THE REALM OF WORDS, WHILE ABSURD WAS OF THE REALM OF LANGUAGE WITHOUT WORDS, AND CAN'T SAY WAS OF THE REALM OF NO MIND, NO WORDS. THE DAO CANNOT BE UNDERSTOOD THROUGH WORDS ALONE.

舜問乎丞曰：「道可得而有乎？」曰：「汝身非汝有也，汝何得有夫道？」舜曰：「吾身非吾有也，孰有之哉？」曰：「是天地之委形也；生非汝有，是天地之委和也；性命非汝有，是天地之委順也；孫子非汝有，是天地之委蛻也。故行不知所往，處不知所持，食不知所味。天地之彊陽氣也，又胡可得而有邪！」

171

東郭子問於莊子曰：「所謂道，惡乎在？」莊子曰：「無所不在。」東郭子曰：「期而後可。」莊子曰：「在螻蟻。」曰：「何其下邪？」曰：「在稊稗。」曰：「何其愈下邪？」曰：「在瓦甓。」曰：「何其愈甚邪？」

172

曰：「在屎溺。」東郭子不應。莊子曰：「夫子之問也，固不及質。正獲之問於監市履豨也，每下愈況。汝唯莫必，無乎逃物。至道若是，大言亦然。周遍咸三者，異名同實，其指一也。」

173

泰清問乎無窮曰：「子知道乎？」無窮曰：「吾不知。」又問乎無為。無為曰：「吾知道。」曰：「子之知道，亦有數乎？」曰：「有。」曰：「其數若何？」無為曰：「吾知道之可以貴，可以賤，可以約，可以散，此吾所以知道之數也。」

泰清以之言也問乎無始曰：「若是，則無窮之弗知與無為之知，孰是而孰非乎？」無始曰：「不知深矣，知之淺矣；弗知內矣，知之外矣。」於是泰清中而歎曰：「弗知乃知乎！知乃不知乎！孰知不知之知？」無始曰：「道不可聞，聞而非也；道不可見，見而非也；道不可言，言而非也。知形形之不形乎！道不當名。」無始曰：「有問道而應之者，不知道也。雖問道者，亦未聞道。」

175

大馬之捶鉤者，年八十矣，而不失豪芒。大馬曰：「子巧與？有道與？」曰：「臣有守也。臣之年二十而好捶鉤，於物無視也，非鉤無察也。是用之者，假不用者也以長得其用，而況乎無不用者乎！物孰不資焉！」

NO DISTRACTIONS

THE MAKER OF BELT HOOKS FOR A HIGH OFFICIAL WAS EIGHTY YEARS OLD, YET HIS PRODUCTS WERE STILL FLAWLESS.

PING PING PING

DO YOU RELY ON SKILL ALONE, OR DO YOU HAVE A CERTAIN METHOD?

I HAVE A METHOD.

WHEN I WAS TWENTY YEARS OLD, I TOOK AN INTEREST IN BELT HOOKS.

FROM THEN ON, I PAID ATTENTION TO NOTHING ELSE.

BY NOT PAYING ATTENTION TO ANYTHING ELSE, I WAS ABLE TO CONCENTRATE ON BELT HOOKS. SO THE USELESSNESS OF OTHER THINGS WAS USEFUL IN THIS WAY.

PING PING PING

WE MUST ALL RECOGNIZE OUR OWN NATURES AND UNDERSTAND WHERE OUR OWN INTERESTS LIE. IF YOU KNOW WHAT YOU REALLY LIKE, NOTHING ELSE WILL ATTRACT YOU, AND YOU CAN CONCENTRATE ON YOUR INTEREST. THIS IS THE REALM OF PERFECTION.

GENGSANG FORSAKES FAME

GENGSANG CHU WAS A VERY ADEPT STUDENT OF LAOZI.

WHILE HE WAS LIVING ON A CLIFF OVERLOOKING THE VILLAGE OF WEI LEI, HARVEST TIME CAME AROUND AND THE VILLAGERS HAD A BUMPER CROP. THEY ATTRIBUTED THEIR GOOD FORTUNE TO GENGSANG CHU OVERSEEING THEM AND SO BEGAN TO WORSHIP AND GIVE THANKS TO HIM. GENGSANG CHU SAID TO HIS DISCIPLES:

IN SPRINGTIME, LEAVES BEGIN TO GROW AND FLOWERS BLOSSOM.

IN THE LATE SUMMER, PLANTS COME TO FRUITION. IT'S THE COURSE OF NATURE! BUT PEOPLE SAY I AM RESPONSIBLE FOR IT JUST BECAUSE I LIVE UP HERE. THEY THINK I AM SOME KIND OF SAGE.

THEREUPON, GENGSANG CHU MOVED AWAY TO THE FOREST.

CHAPTER 23
GENGSANG CHU

老聃之役有庚桑楚者，偏得老聃之道，以北居畏壘之山⋯⋯。居三年，畏壘大壤。畏壘之民相與言曰：「庚桑子之始來，吾洒然異之。今吾日計之而不足，歲計之而有餘。庶幾其聖人乎！子胡不相與尸而祝之，社而稷之乎？」⋯⋯庚桑子曰：「⋯⋯夫春氣發而百草生，正得秋而萬寶成。夫春與秋，豈無得而然哉？天道已行矣。吾聞至人，尸居環堵之室，而百姓猖狂不知所如往。今以畏壘之細民而竊竊焉欲俎豆予于賢人之閒，我其杓之人邪！吾是以不釋於老聃之言。」

177

學者，學其所不能學也；行者，行其所不能行也；辯者，辯其所不能辯也。知止乎其所不能知，至矣；若有不即是者，天鈞敗之。

BREAKING BARRIERS

A STUDENT STUDIES WHAT HE CAN'T STUDY.

A DO-ER DOES WHAT HE CAN'T DO.

A DEBATER DEBATES WHAT HE CAN'T DEBATE.

A KNOWLEDGE-SEEKER SET HIS SIGHTS ON WHAT HE CAN'T KNOW.

IF THIS WEREN'T THE CASE, NATURAL EQUANIMITY WOULD BE LOST.

THE NATURE OF NATURE IS CONSTANT CHANGE. IF YOU DO THE SAME THINGS OR STUDY THE SAME THINGS OVER AND OVER, HOW ARE YOU DIFFERENT FROM A CORPSE?

ULTIMATE BENEVOLENCE

OOOPS, I'M SORRY! PLEASE EXCUSE ME!

OW!

IF YOU STEP ON A STRANGER'S FOOT, YOU MUST APOLOGIZE AND SHOW REMORSE.

OOOPS, ARE YOU OKAY?

OW!

IF YOU STEP ON YOUR OLDER BROTHER'S FOOT, YOU MUST COMFORT HIM A BIT.

IF YOU STEP ON YOUR FATHER'S FOOT, YOU DON'T HAVE TO DO ANYTHING.

LOVE IS NEVER HAVING TO SAY YOU'RE SORRY!

OW!

ULTIMATE PROPRIETY IS TO NOT DISTINGUISH BETWEEN SELF AND OTHER; ULTIMATE RIGHTEOUSNESS IS TO NOT DISTINGUISH BETWEEN SELF AND THINGS; ULTIMATE WISDOM IS TO NOT SCHEME; ULTIMATE BENEVOLENCE IS TO NOT DISTINGUISH BETWEEN REMOTE AND INTIMATE; ULTIMATE TRUST DOES NOT SEEK VALUABLES AS COLLATERAL.

蹍市人之足，則辭以放驚，兄則以嫗，大親則已矣。

故曰：至禮有不人，至義不物，至知不謀，至仁無親，至信辟金。

CHAPTER 24
Xu Wugui

徐無鬼因女商見魏武侯，武侯勞之曰：「先生病矣！苦於山林之勞，故乃肯見於寡人。」徐無鬼曰：「我則勞於君，君有何勞於我！君將盈嗜欲，長好惡，則性命之情病矣；君將黜嗜欲，掔好惡，則耳目病矣。我將勞君，君有何勞於我！」武侯超然不對。

少焉，徐無鬼曰：「嘗語君，吾相狗也。下之質執飽而止，是狸德也；

181

武侯大悅而笑。

中之質若視日，上之質若亡其一。吾相狗，又不若吾相馬也。吾相馬，直者中繩，曲者中鉤，方者中矩，圓者中規，是國馬也，而未若天下馬也。天下馬有成材，若卹若失，若喪其一，若是者，超軼絕塵，不知其所。」

A MEDIUM-GRADE DOG HAS BRIGHT EYES AND ACTS SUPERIOR TO OTHERS.

A HIGH-GRADE DOG IS SO CALM AND COMPOSED IT EVEN FORGETS IT'S A DOG!

HA HA HA! WELL SAID, WELL SAID.

I'M EVEN BETTER AT APPRAISING HORSES. THERE ARE TWO KINDS OF HORSE: THE STATE HORSE AND THE WORLD HORSE.

WHAT'S A STATE HORSE?

REGARDLESS OF ITS TEETH, BACK, HEAD, OR EYES, IF A HORSE OBEYS THE BRIDLE AND REINS AND ACTS COMPLETELY WITHIN THE CONFINES OF ITS TRAINING, IT IS A STATE HORSE.

WHAT'S A WORLD HORSE, THEN?

A WORLD HORSE HAS AN INNATE CHARACTER. IT IS SO SERENE THAT IT SEEMS TO FORGET ITS OWN BODY. AND WHEN THIS KIND OF HORSE RUNS, IT NEARLY FLIES. THAT'S WHAT A WORLD HORSE IS.

WONDERFUL, WONDERFUL! YOU KNOW YOUR HORSES, ALL RIGHT!

徐無鬼出，女商曰：「先生獨何以說吾君乎？吾所以說吾君者，橫說之則以《詩》、《書》、《禮》、《樂》，從說之則以《金板》、《六弢》，奉事而大有功者不可為數，而吾君未嘗啟齒。今先生何以說吾君，使吾君悅若此乎？」徐無鬼曰：「吾直告之吾相狗馬耳。」女商曰：「若是乎？」曰：「子不聞夫越之流人乎？去國數日，見其所知而喜；

183

去國旬月，見所嘗見於國中者喜；及期年也，見似人者而喜矣，不亦去人滋久，思人滋深乎？夫逃虛空者，藜藋柱乎鼪鼬之逕，跟位其空，聞人足音跫然而喜矣，有況乎昆弟親戚之謦欬其側者乎！久矣夫！莫以真人之言謦欬吾君之側乎！」

184

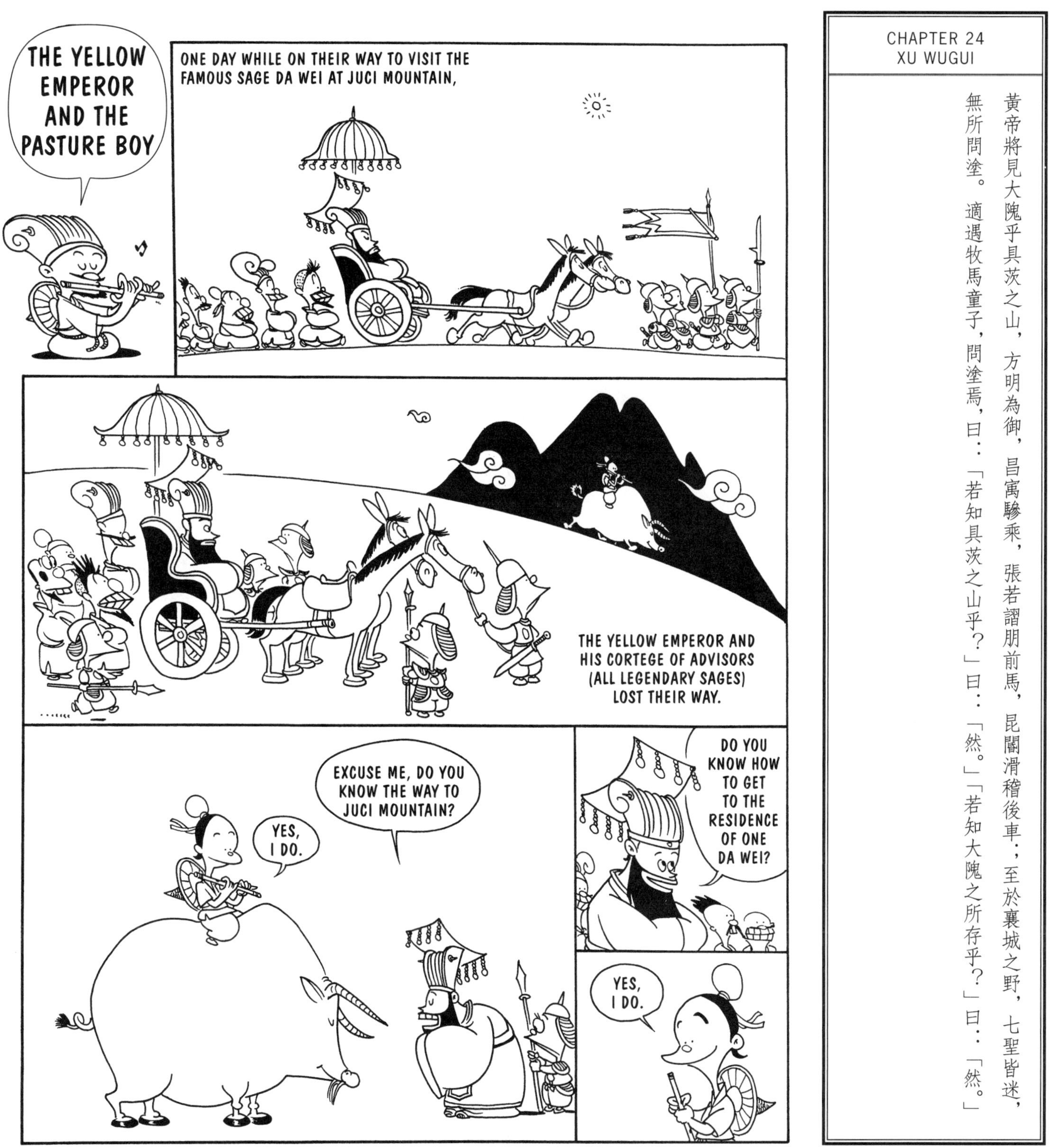
THE YELLOW EMPEROR AND THE PASTURE BOY
ONE DAY WHILE ON THEIR WAY TO VISIT THE FAMOUS SAGE DA WEI AT JUCI MOUNTAIN,
THE YELLOW EMPEROR AND HIS CORTEGE OF ADVISORS (ALL LEGENDARY SAGES) LOST THEIR WAY.
EXCUSE ME, DO YOU KNOW THE WAY TO JUCI MOUNTAIN?
YES, I DO.
DO YOU KNOW HOW TO GET TO THE RESIDENCE OF ONE DA WEI?
YES, I DO.

CHAPTER 24
XU WUGUI

黃帝將見大隗乎具茨之山，方明為御，昌寓驂乘，張若謵朋前馬，昆閽滑稽後車；至於襄城之野，七聖皆迷，無所問塗。適遇牧馬童子，問塗焉，曰：「若知具茨之山乎？」曰：「然。」「若知大隗之所存乎？」曰：「然。」

黃帝曰：「異哉小童！非徒知具茨之山，又知大隗之所存。請問為天下。」……小童曰：「夫為天下者，亦

奚以異乎牧馬者哉！亦去其害馬者而已矣！」黃帝再拜稽首，稱天師而退。

STRANGE, NOT ONLY DO YOU KNOW OF JUCI MOUNTAIN, BUT YOU ALSO KNOW WHO DA WEI IS.

WELL THEN, DO YOU HAPPEN TO KNOW HOW TO RULE THE LAND, TOO?

YES, I DO.

RULING THE LAND IS LIKE WATCHING AFTER HORSES. JUST GET RID OF ANYTHING THAT MIGHT HARM THE ORIGINAL NATURE OF THE HORSES.

THANK YOU SO MUCH! YOU ARE TRULY WISE.

IT WASN'T UNTIL AFTER LISTENING TO THE PASTURE BOY THAT THE YELLOW EMPEROR AND HIS ADVISORS REALIZED THAT THEY HAD ALREADY REACHED THEIR DESTINATION. SO, JUST WHO WAS THAT PASTURE BOY?

莊子送葬，過惠子之墓，顧謂從者曰：「郢人堊漫其鼻端若蠅翼，使匠石斲之。匠石運斤成風，聽而斲之，盡堊而鼻不傷，郢人立不失容。

187

宋元君聞之，召匠石曰：『嘗試為寡人為之。』匠石曰：『臣則嘗能斲之。雖然，臣之質死久矣。』自夫子之死也，吾無以為質矣，吾無與言之矣。」

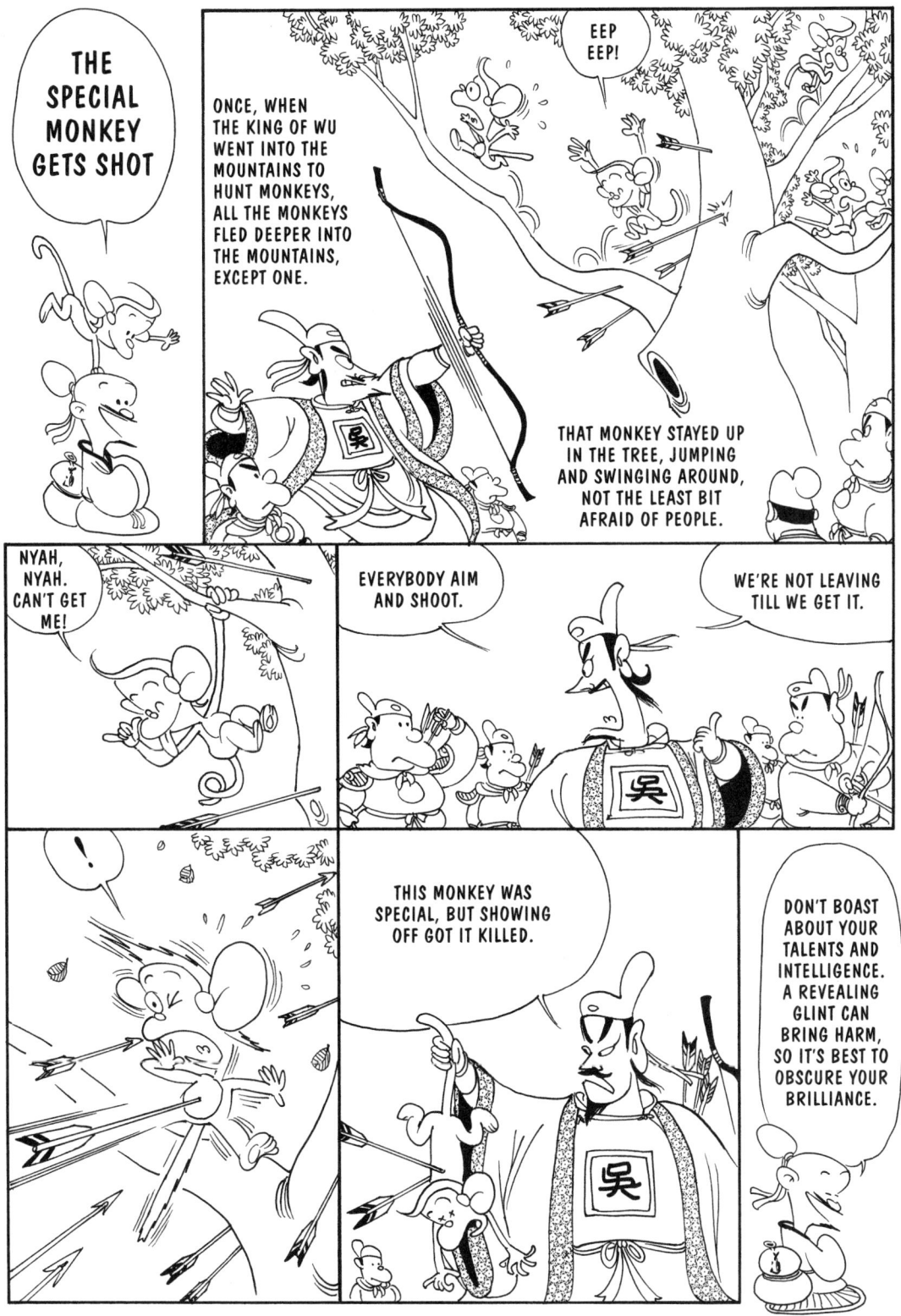

吳王浮于江，登乎狙之山。眾狙見之，恂然棄而走，逃於深蓁。有一狙焉，委蛇攫搔，見巧乎王。王射之，敏給搏捷矢。王命相者趨射之，狙執死。王顧謂其友顏不疑曰：「之狙也，伐其巧恃其便以敖予，以至此殛也！嗟乎，無以汝色驕人哉！」顏不疑歸而師董梧以鋤其色，去樂辭顯，三年而國人稱之。戒之哉！

故足之於地也踐，雖踐，恃其所不蹍而後善博也；人之知也少，雖少，恃其所不知而後知天之所謂也。知大一，知大陰，知大目，知大均，知大方，知大信，知大定，至矣。大一通之，大陰解之，大目視之，大均緣之，大方體之，大信稽之，大定持之。盡有天，循有照，冥有樞，始有彼。則其解之也似不解之者，其知之也似不知之也，不知而後知之。

THE REALM OF IGNORANCE

YOUR FOOT ONLY NEEDS A PIECE OF GROUND THE SIZE OF YOUR SHOE, BUT TO GO ANY DISTANCE, YOU ALSO DEPEND ON THE GROUND THAT THE FEET DON'T WALK ON.

WE ONLY KNOW SO MUCH, AND YET IT IS BY RELYING ON THAT WHICH WE DON'T KNOW THAT WE CAN COME TO UNDERSTAND NATURE.

PERFECTION IS REALIZING:

THE GRAND UNITY,
THE GRAND MYSTERY,
THE GRAND VISION,
THE GRAND EQUANIMITY,
THE GRAND MAGNANIMITY,
THE GRAND TRUST,
AND
THE GRAND SERENITY.

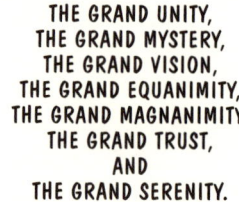

TO REALIZE THE GRAND UNITY IS TO UNDERSTAND THE DAO,
TO REALIZE THE GRAND MYSTERY IS TO UNRAVEL THE MYSTERY OF THE DAO,
TO REALIZE THE GRAND VISION IS TO SEE THE DAO,
TO REALIZE THE GRAND EQUANIMITY IS TO FLOW WITH THE DAO,
TO REALIZE THE GRAND MAGNANIMITY IS TO EXPERIENCE THE DAO,
TO REALIZE THE GRAND TRUST IS FIND THE TRUTH IN THE DAO,
TO REALIZE THE GRAND SERENITY IS TO MAINTAIN THE DAO.

WE SHOULD ALL FOLLOW NATURE, BE IN ACCORDANCE WITH THE MYRIAD THINGS, CONCEAL THE DAOIST MIND, AND UNDERSTAND OURSELVES AND OTHERS.

IN THIS KIND OF REALM, RESOLVING THE MYSTERY OF THE DAO IS LIKE THE TIME BEFORE IT WAS RESOLVED, AND REALIZING THE DAO IS LIKE THE TIME BEFORE IT WAS REALIZED— KNOWLEDGE COMES ONLY AFTER RECOGNIZING OUR IGNORANCE.

冉相氏得其環中以隨成，與物無終無始，無幾無時。日與物化者，一不化者也，闔嘗舍之！大師天而不得師天，與物皆殉，其以為事也若之何？

THE CYCLIC DAO

THE GREAT SAGE RANXIANG REALIZED THE SIGNIFICANCE OF THE CYCLE AND HOW IT IS A SEQUENTIAL COMPOSITION OF UNCEASING TRANSFORMATIONS.

FOR ANY PARTICULAR THING, THERE IS NO BRIGHT LINE SEPARATING PAST, PRESENT, AND FUTURE.

THE BODY BECOMES ONE WITH THE MYRIAD THINGS, AND THE GENUINE SELF DOESN'T LEAVE EVEN FOR A MOMENT. NATURE IS EMULATED, BUT NOT INTENTIONALLY. THERE ISN'T EVEN AN IDEA OF NATURE OR OF PEOPLE.

THE DAO IS WITHOUT BEGINNING OR END, WITHOUT A MOTIVE FORCE, AND WITHOUT TIME. TO BE IN ACCORD WITH IT, WE FOLLOW THE MYRIAD THINGS ON THEIR CYCLIC PATH, FOREVER CHANGING AND FOREVER TRANQUIL.

191

魏瑩與田侯牟約，田侯牟背之。魏瑩怒，將使人刺之……。戴晉人曰：「有所謂蝸者，君知之乎？」曰：「然。」「有國於蝸之左角者曰觸氏，有國於蝸之右角者曰蠻氏，時相與爭地而戰，伏尸數萬，逐北旬有五日而後反。」君曰：「噫！其虛言與？」曰：「臣請為君實之。君以意在四方上下有窮乎？」君曰：「無窮。」曰：「知遊心於無窮，而反在通達之國，若存若亡乎？」君曰：「然。」曰：「通達之中有魏，於魏中有梁，於梁中有王。王與蠻氏，有辯乎？」

192

莊周家貧，故往貸粟於監河侯。監河侯曰：「諾。我將得邑金，將貸子三百金，可乎？」莊周忿然作色曰：

「周昨來，有中道而呼者。周顧視，車轍中有鮒魚焉。周問之曰：『鮒魚來，子何為者邪？』對曰：『我，東海之波臣也。君豈有斗升之水而活我哉？』周曰：『諾。我且南遊吳越之王，激西江之水而迎子，可乎？』鮒魚忿然作色曰：『吾失我常與，我無所處。吾得斗升之水然活耳，君乃言此，曾不如早索我於枯魚之肆！』」

其於得大魚難矣，飾小說以干縣令，其於大達亦遠矣，是以未嘗聞任氏之風俗，其不可與經於世亦遠矣。

河以東，蒼梧已北，莫不厭若魚者。已而後世輇才諷說之徒，皆驚而相告也。夫揭竿累，趨灌瀆，守鯢鮒，

鈎錎沒而下，驚揚而奮鬐，白波若山，海水震蕩，聲侔鬼神，憚赫千里。任公子得若魚，離而腊之，自制

任公子為大鈎巨緇，五十犗以為餌，蹲乎會稽，投竿東海，旦旦而釣，期年不得魚。已而大魚食之，牽巨

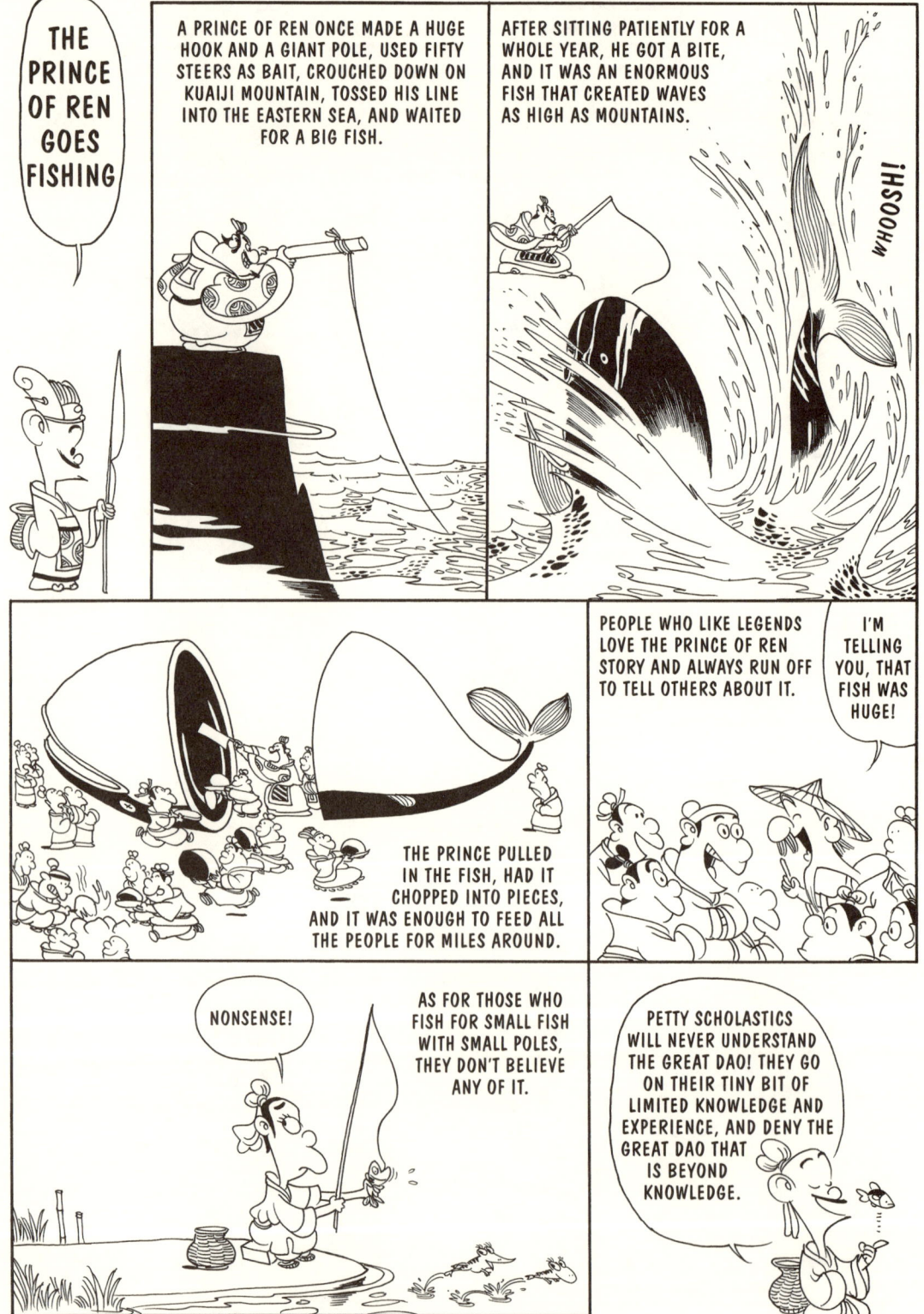

宋元君夜半而夢人被髮闚阿門，曰：「予自宰路之淵，予為清江使河伯之所，漁者余且得予。」元君覺，使人占之，曰：「此神龜也。」君曰：「漁者有余且乎？」左右曰：「有。」君曰：「令余且會朝。」明日，余且朝。君曰：「漁何得？」對曰：「且之網得白龜焉，其圓五尺。」君曰：「獻若之龜。」

龜至，君再欲殺之，再欲活之，心疑，卜之，曰：「殺龜以卜吉。」乃刳龜，七十二鑽而無遺筴。仲尼曰：「神龜能見夢於元君，而不能避余且之網；知能七十二鑽而無遺筴，不能避刳腸之患。如是，則知有所困，神有所不及也。雖有至知，萬人謀之。魚不畏網而畏鵜鶘。去小知而大知明，去善而自善矣。」

NATURAL USE

ONE DAY, ZHUANGZI LECTURED HUIZI HOUR UPON HOUR ABOUT THE DAO.

INCONSEQUENTIAL!

TRIVIAL!

EVERYTHING YOU'VE SAID IS COMPLETELY USELESS!

GOOD. NOW THAT YOU UNDERSTAND USELESSNESS, WE CAN TALK ABOUT USEFULNESS.

FOR INSTANCE, YOU'RE REALLY ONLY USING THIS LITTLE PIECE OF GROUND YOU'RE STANDING ON, RIGHT?

AHHH!

THEREFORE: USEFULNESS IS BUILT ON A FOUNDATION OF USELESSNESS. IF THERE IS NO USELESSNESS, THEN THERE IS NO USEFULNESS.

BUT, IF WE CUT AWAY ALL THE REST OF THE GROUND AROUND IT...

HOW USEFUL IS IT?

USEFUL

USELESS USELESS USELESS USELESS USELESS USELESS USELESS USELESS USELESS USELESS USELESS USELESS

惠子謂莊子曰：「子言無用。」莊子曰：「知無用而始可與言用矣。夫地非不廣且大也，人之所用容足耳。然則廁足而墊之致黃泉，人尚有用乎？」惠子曰：「無用。」莊子曰：「然則無用之為用也亦明矣。」

197

荃者所以在魚，得魚而忘荃；蹄者所以在兔，得兔而忘蹄；言者所以在意，得意而忘言。吾安得夫忘言之人而與之言哉！

CATCH THE FISH, DISCARD THE TRAP

SOME PEOPLE CATCH FISH WITH TRAPS.

AFTER CATCHING THE FISH, THE TRAP CAN BE DISCARDED.

JUST LIKE SNARES FOR CATCHING RABBITS.

AFTER CATCHING YOUR RABBIT, THE SNARE CAN BE FORGOTTEN.

LANGUAGE IS THE SAME WAY.

AFTER THE MEANING HAS BEEN TRANSMITTED, THE WORDS CAN BE DISPENSED WITH.

LANGUAGE IS A MEANS, NOT AN END. WHAT'S THE DIFFERENCE BETWEEN GOING STRICTLY BY THE BOOK (EVEN TO THE POINT OF EXHAUSTIVELY STUDYING THE CLASSICS) AND "CONCENTRATING ON THE BRANCHES IN NEGLECT OF THE ROOTS"?

CONFUCIUS CHANGES

WHEN CONFUCIUS HAD LIVED FOR SIXTY YEARS, HE HAD ALSO CHANGED FOR SIXTY YEARS

WHAT HE HAD THOUGHT WAS WRONG IN THE PAST HE MIGHT HAVE THOUGHT TO BE RIGHT IN THE PRESENT. WHAT HE THOUGHT TO BE WRONG IN THE PRESENT HE MIGHT HAVE THOUGHT WAS RIGHT IN THE PAST.

HUIZI ASKED ZHUANGZI:

DID CONFUCIUS WORK HARD TO FULFILL HIS AMBITIONS AND PUT HIS KNOWLEDGE TO USE?

CONFUCIUS WAS BEYOND THAT.

HE FELT THAT, ALTHOUGH DEBATING RIGHT AND WRONG COULD WIN VERBAL ASSENT, IT COULDN'T WIN PEOPLE'S HEARTS. IF YOU WANT TO WIN PEOPLE'S HEARTS, YOU MUST ACT IN ACCORDANCE WITH THE NATURAL DAO.

PUTTING INTELLIGENCE TO USE IS A LOWER LEVEL. A WISE PERSON GOES BEYOND IT.

CHAPTER 27
ASCRIPTIONS

莊子謂惠子曰：「孔子行年六十而六十化，始時所是，卒而非之，未知今之所謂是之非五十九非也。」惠子曰：「孔子勤志服知也。」莊子曰：「孔子謝之矣，而其未之嘗言？孔子云：『夫受才乎大本，復靈以生，』鳴而當律，言而當法，利義陳乎前，而好惡是非直服人之口而已矣。使人乃以心服，而不敢蘁立，定天下之定。已乎已乎！吾且不得及彼乎！」

199

曾子再仕而心再化，曰：「吾及親仕，三釜而心樂；後仕，三千鍾不洎，吾心悲。」弟子問于仲尼曰：「若參者，可謂無所縣其罪乎？」曰：「既已縣矣。夫無所縣者，可以有哀乎？彼視三釜三千鍾，如觀雀蚊虻相過乎前也。」

NO ATTACHMENTS

THE SECOND TIME ZENGZI WORKED AS AN OFFICIAL, HE EXPERIENCED A CHANGE OF ATTITUDE...

BEFORE, WHEN I WAS AN OFFICIAL, MY SALARY WAS ONLY FIVE PECKS OF GRAIN, AND YET I WAS VERY HAPPY —BECAUSE MY PARENTS WERE ALIVE THEN.

NOW MY SALARY IS FIFTEEN THOUSAND BUSHELS, AND I FEEL JUST TERRIBLE.

MASTER, CAN A PERSON LIKE ZENGZI BE CONSIDERED TO HAVE NO ATTACHMENTS?

HE ISN'T ATTACHED TO HIS SALARY, BUT HE DOES HAVE ATTACHMENTS. DOES A PERSON WITH NO ATTACHMENTS FEEL HAPPINESS OR SADNESS?

A PERSON WITH NO ATTACHMENTS VIEWS A SALARY OF FIVE PECKS OR FIFTEEN THOUSAND BUSHELS AS HE WOULD A SPARROW OR A MOSQUITO PASSING BY.

ZENGZI MAY NOT HAVE BEEN ATTACHED TO HIS SALARY, BUT HE HAD CERTAINLY BEEN ATTACHED TO HIS PARENTS, AND THIS IS WHY HE FELT SAD. ANYONE WHO HAS FEELINGS OF HAPPINESS OR SADNESS HAS ATTACHMENTS.

顏成子游謂東郭子綦曰：「自吾聞子之言，一年而野，二年而從，三年而通，四年而物，五年而來，六年而鬼入，七年而天成，八年而不知死，不知生，九年而大妙。

201

陽子居南之沛，老聃西遊於秦，邀於郊，至於梁而遇老子。老子中道仰天而歎曰：「始以汝為可教，今不可也。」陽子居不荅。至舍，進盥漱巾櫛，脫屨戶外，膝行而前曰：「向者弟子欲請夫子，夫子行不閒，是以不敢。今閒矣，請問其過。」老子曰：「而睢睢盱盱，而誰與居？大白若辱，盛德若不足。」陽子居蹴然變容曰：「敬聞命矣！」其往也，舍者迎將，其家公執席，妻執巾櫛，舍者避席，煬者避灶。其反也，舍者與之爭席矣。

堯以天下讓許由，許由不受。又讓於子州支父，子州支父曰：「以我為天子，猶之可也。雖然，我適有幽憂之病，方且治之，未暇治天下也。」夫天下至重也，而不以害其生，又況他物乎！唯無以天下為者，可以託天下也。

LIFE IS MOST IMPORTANT

EMPEROR YAO WISHED TO ABDICATE AND HAND THE WORLD OVER TO XU YOU, BUT XU YOU WOULDN'T ACCEPT...

SO YAO ASKED ZIZHOU ZHIFU...

I WOULD ACCEPT...

BUT I HAVE A VERY WORRISOME ILLNESS. BECAUSE I'VE GOT TO GET THAT CURED, I'M AFRAID I WON'T HAVE TIME TO GOVERN THE LAND.

EMPEROR IS THE MOST POWERFUL POSITION IN THE WORLD, BUT THERE ARE SOME WHO WOULD REFUSE TO EXCHANGE THEIR LIVES FOR IT. THIS IS WHAT SEPARATES A PERSON OF THE DAO FROM A COMMON PERSON.

楚昭王失國，屠羊說走而從於昭王。昭王反國，將賞從者，及屠羊說。屠羊說曰：「大王失國，說失屠羊，大王反國，說亦反屠羊。臣之爵祿已復矣，又何賞之有！」王曰：「強之！」屠羊說曰：「大王失國，非臣之罪，故不敢伏其誅；大王反國，非臣之功，故不敢當其賞。」

THE GOAT-BUTCHER REFUSES REWARD

WHEN KING ZHAO OF CHU LOST HIS COUNTRY, YUE THE GOAT-BUTCHER FLED WITH HIM. AFTER THE WU ARMY RETREATED AND KING ZHAO RETURNED...

THE KING WOULD LIKE TO REWARD THOSE WHO ENDURED HARDSHIPS WITH HIM. YOU ARE ONE.

GOAT MEAT

WHEN THE KING FLED, I ALSO ABANDONED MY BUSINESS. NOW HE HAS RETURNED, AND I AM BUTCHERING GOATS AGAIN, SO WHAT'S TO BE REWARDED?

YOU WENT THROUGH A LOT WITH THE KING, AND HE'D LIKE YOU TO ACCEPT A SMALL TOKEN OF HIS APPRECIATION.

I DIDN'T CAUSE HIM TO FLEE OR RETURN, SO I DON'T THINK I SHOULD BE PUNISHED OR REWARDED.

SOCIETY'S PRAISE AND BLAME ARE USUALLY JUST MUTUAL DECEPTION. IF YOU CAN SEE THROUGH THIS, YOU WILL BE WITHOUT ANY OBSTACLES WHATSOEVER, AND YOUR MIND WILL BE PURE AND CAREFREE.

ZIGONG'S SNOW-WHITE CLOTHES

YUAN XIAN AND ZIGONG WERE STUDENTS OF CONFUCIUS.

YUAN XIAN WAS VERY POOR. HE LIVED IN A HOUSE WHERE THE ROOF LEAKED...

AND THERE WAS A BIG HOLE IN ONE OF THE WALLS. BUT HE DIDN'T MIND.

BEING A GOOD SPEAKER, ZIGONG BECAME A HIGH OFFICIAL AND WAS VERY PROUD OF HIMSELF. ONE DAY HE PAID A VISIT TO YUAN XIAN.

THE LANE IS TOO NARROW, SIR. THE CARRIAGE WON'T FIT.

原憲居魯，環堵之室，茨以生草：蓬戶不完，桑以為樞：而甕牖二室，褐以為塞：上漏下濕，匡坐而弦。子貢乘大馬，中紺而表素，軒車不容巷，往見原憲。原憲華冠縱履，杖藜而應門。

子貢曰：「嘻！先生何病？」原憲應之曰：「憲聞之，無財謂之貧，學而不能行謂之病。今憲貧也，非病也。」子貢逡巡而有愧色。原憲笑曰：「夫希世而行，比周而友，學以為人，教以為己，仁義之慝，輿馬之飾，憲不忍為也。」

孔子謂顏回曰：「回，來！家貧居卑，胡不仕乎？」顏回對曰：「不願仕。回有郭外之田五十畝，足以給饘粥；郭內之田十畝，足以為絲麻；鼓琴足以自娛，所學夫子之道者足以自樂也。回不願仕。」孔子愀然變容曰：「善哉，回之意！丘聞之，『知足者不以利自累也，審自得者失之而不懼，行脩於內者無位而不怍。』丘誦之久矣，今於回而後見之，是丘之得也。」

207

孔子與柳下季為友，柳下季之弟名曰盜跖。盜跖從卒九千人，橫行天下，侵暴諸侯，穴室樞戶，驅人牛馬，取人婦女，貪得忘親，不顧父母兄弟，不祭先祖。所過之邑，大國守城，小國入保，萬民苦之。孔子謂柳下季曰：

「夫為人父者，必能詔其子；為人兄者，必能教其弟。若父不能詔其子，兄不能教其弟，則無貴父子兄弟之親矣。今先生，世之才士也，弟為盜跖，為天下害，而弗能教也，丘竊為先生羞之。丘請為先生往說之。」柳下季曰：

「……且跖之為人也，心如涌泉，意如飄風，強足以距敵，辯足以飾非，順其心則喜，逆其心則怒，易辱人以言。先生必無往。」

THE BANDIT SPEAKS

LIUXIA JI WAS A FRIEND OF CONFUCIUS AND HAD A LITTLE BROTHER KNOWN AS ZHI THE BANDIT. ZHI HAD NINE THOUSAND FOLLOWERS AND TOGETHER THEY RAVAGED THE LAND.

PARENTS SHOULD TEACH THEIR CHILDREN, AND OLDER BROTHERS SHOULD TEACH THEIR YOUNGER BROTHERS. YOUR LITTLE BROTHER IS A TERRIBLE VILLAIN AND RAVAGES THE LAND. ISN'T THERE ANYTHING YOU CAN DO?

WHAT CAN I DO? SOME PEOPLE JUST DON'T LISTEN.

WELL, THEN LET ME HAVE A TRY!

LOOK, MY BROTHER HAS A BAD TEMPER. IF YOU CROSS HIM, I CAN'T SAY WHAT MIGHT HAPPEN. I THINK IT WOULD BE BETTER IF YOU DIDN'T GO.

CONFUCIUS DISREGARDED THE WARNING, AND WITH HIS DISCIPLES ZIGONG AND YAN HUI, HE WENT TO SEE ZHI THE BANDIT.

GENERAL, CONFUCIUS IS OUTSIDE. HE WANTS TO SEE YOU.

RRRR! RRRRRR!

TAKE A MESSAGE TO HIM. TELL HIM TO STOP CONFUSING RIGHT AND WRONG AND STOP MEDDLING IN THE AFFAIRS OF THE LAND'S KINGS AND PRINCES.

TELL HIM TO STOP CHEATING PEOPLE THROUGH HIS SUPPOSED MORALITY IN ORDER TO GAIN UNDESERVED WEALTH AND RANK. HIS SINS ARE GREAT. TELL HIM THAT IF HE HURRIES, HE CAN ESCAPE DOWN THE MOUNTAIN BEFORE I GET HIM!

OTHERWISE, I'LL HAVE HIS HEART AND LIVER FOR LUNCH!

YES, SIR.

孔子不聽，顏回為馭，子貢為右，往見盜跖。盜跖乃方休卒徒太山之陽，膾人肝而餔之。孔子下車而前，見謁者曰：「魯人孔丘，聞將軍高義，敬再拜謁者。」謁者入通，盜跖聞之大怒，目如明星，髮上指冠，曰：「此夫魯國之巧偽人孔丘非邪？為我告之：『爾作言造語，妄稱文武，冠枝木之冠，帶死牛之脅，多辭謬說，不耕而食，不織而衣，搖脣鼓舌，擅生是非，以迷天下之主，使天下學士不反其本，妄作孝悌而僥倖於封侯富貴者也。子之罪大極重，疾走歸！不然，我將以子肝益晝餔之膳！』」

209

孔子復通曰：「丘得幸於季，願望履幕下。」謁者復通，盜跖……曰：「丘來前！若所言，順吾意則生，逆吾心則死。」孔子曰：「丘聞之，凡天下有三德，生而長大，美好無雙，少長貴賤見而皆悅之，此上德也；知維天地，能辯諸物，此中德也；勇悍果敢，聚眾率兵，此下德也。凡人有此一德者，足以南面稱孤矣。今將軍兼此三者，身長八尺二寸，面目有光，脣如激丹，齒如齊貝，音中黃鍾，而名曰盜跖，丘竊為將軍恥不取焉。

將軍有意聽臣，臣請南使吳越，北使齊魯，東使宋衛，西使晉楚，使為將軍造大城數百里，立數十萬戶之邑，尊將軍為諸侯，與天下更始，罷兵休卒，收養昆弟，共祭先祖。此聖人才士之行，而天下之願也。」盜跖大怒，曰：「……今丘告我以大城眾民，是欲規我以利而恆民畜我也，安可長久也！城之大者，莫大乎天下矣。堯舜有天下，子孫無置錐之地；湯武立為天子，而後世絕滅；非以其利大故邪？

丘之所言，皆吾之所棄也，亟去走歸，無復言之！子之道，狂狂汲汲，詐巧虛偽事也，非可以全真也，奚足論哉！」孔子再拜趨走，出門上車，執轡三失，目芒然無見，色若死灰，不能出氣。歸到魯東門外，適遇柳下季。柳下季曰：「今者闕然數日不見，車馬有行色，得微往見跖邪？」孔子仰天而歎曰：「然。」柳下季曰：「跖得無逆汝意若前乎？」孔子曰：「然。丘所謂無病而自灸也，疾走料虎頭，編虎須，幾不免虎口哉！」

SO, TAKE YOUR OFFER AND HIT THE ROAD. I'LL HAVE NOTHING TO DO WITH THAT KIND OF HYPOCRISY. IT'S TOO FAR FROM THE DAO!

OH MY! OH MY! OH MY...

I RUSHED TO PULL THE TIGER'S BEARD AND ALMOST GOT EATEN.

MY BROTHER DIDN'T OFFEND YOU, DID HE?

OF COURSE, CONFUCIUS WAS NOT A HYPOCRITE HIMSELF, BUT HOW MANY OF OUR LEADERS DO HARM IN THE NAME OF GOOD?

昔趙文王喜劍，劍士夾門而客三千餘人，日夜相擊於前，死傷者歲百餘人，好之不厭。如是三年，國衰，諸侯謀之。太子悝患之，募左右曰：「孰能說王之意止劍士者，賜之千金。」左右曰：「莊子當能。」太子乃使人以千金奉莊子……。莊子曰：「聞太子所欲用周者，欲絕王之喜好也。」

213

臣之劍，十步一人，千里不留行。」

「子欲何以教寡人，使太子先？」曰：

「臣聞大王喜劍，故以劍見王。」王曰：

「子之劍何能禁制？」曰：

「請治劍服。」治劍服三日，乃見太子。太子乃與見王，王脫白刃待之。莊子入殿門不趨，見王不拜。王曰：

「子欲何以教寡人，使太子先？」曰：

太子曰：「然。吾王所見，唯劍士也。」莊子曰：「諾。周善為劍。」太子曰：「然。吾王所見劍士，皆蓬頭突鬢垂冠，曼胡之纓，短後之衣，瞋目而語難，王乃悅之。今夫子必儒服而見王，事必大逆。」莊子曰：

GET ME AN AUDIENCE WITH THE KING.

I WOULD, BUT HE WON'T SEE ANYONE BUT SWORDFIGHTERS.

NO PROBLEM— I HAPPEN TO KNOW A BIT ABOUT SWORD FIGHTING MYSELF.

THE KING ONLY LIKES THE BIG UGLY TYPE WITH MESSY HAIR AND RASPY VOICES, MEN WHOSE EYES LOOK LIKE THEY BELONG ON A DEAD FISH; YOU'RE NOT LIKE THAT.

JUST GET ME SOME SWORDFIGHTER'S GEAR, AND I'LL TAKE CARE OF THE REST.

YOU'RE A GOOD SWORDFIGHTER? HOW DID YOU PERSUADE THE PRINCE TO GET AN AUDIENCE WITH ME?

I'M SO GOOD THAT THERE ISN'T A PERSON WITHIN A THOUSAND MILES WHO COULD BEAT ME. IF SOMEONE EVEN TRIED TO FIGHT ME, HE WOULDN'T GET WITHIN TEN FEET OF ME BEFORE I STRUCK HIM DOWN.

王大悅之，曰：「天下無敵矣！」莊子曰：「夫為劍者，示之以虛，開之以利，後之以發，先之以至。願得試之。」王曰：「夫子休，就舍。待命令設戲請夫子。」王乃校劍士七日，死傷者六十餘人，得五六人，使奉劍於殿下，乃召莊子。

215

CHAPTER 30
PERSUASION WITH SWORDS

王曰：「今日試使士敦劍。」莊子曰：「望之久矣。」王曰：「夫子所御杖，長短何如？」曰：「臣之所奉皆可。然臣有三劍，唯王所用，請先言而後試。」王曰：「願聞三劍。」曰：「有天子劍，有諸侯劍，有庶人劍。」王曰：「天子之劍何如？」曰：「天子之劍，以燕谿石城為鋒，齊岱為鍔，晉魏為脊，周宋為鐔，韓魏為鋏；包以四夷，裹以四時，繞以渤海，帶以常山；制以五行，論以刑德，開以陰陽，持以春夏，行以秋冬。

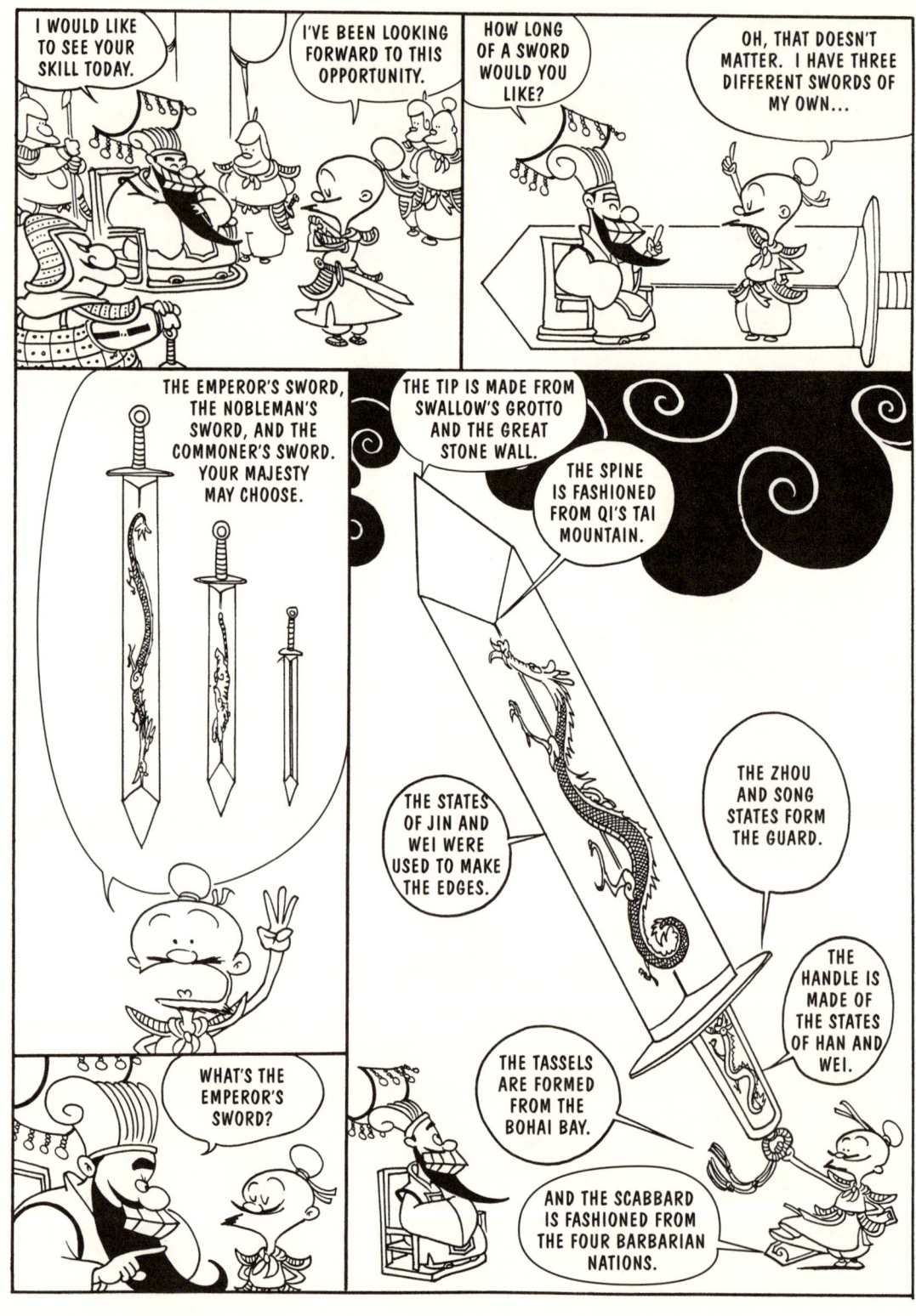

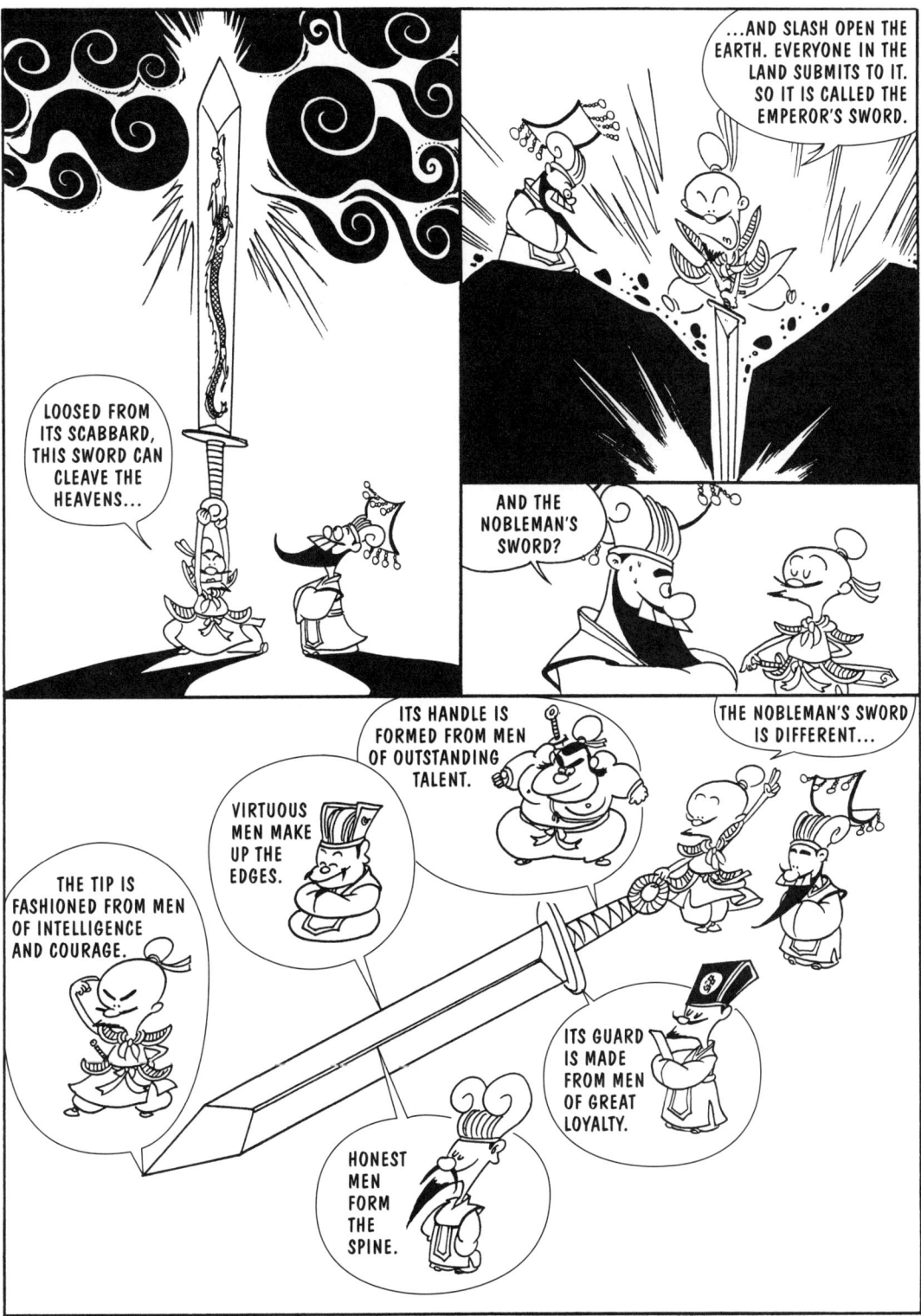

此劍，直之無前，舉之無上，案之無下，運之無旁，上決浮雲，下絕地紀。此劍一用，匡諸侯，天下服矣。此天子之劍也。」文王芒然自失，曰：「諸侯之劍何如？」曰：「諸侯之劍，以知勇士為鋒，以清廉士為鍔，以賢良士為脊，以忠聖士為鐔，以豪桀士為鋏。

217

此劍，直之亦無前，舉之亦無上，案之亦無下，運之亦無旁，上法圓天以順三光，下法方地以順四時，中

和民意以安四鄉。此劍一用，如雷霆之震也，四封之內，無不賓服而聽從君命者矣。此諸侯之劍也。」王

曰：「庶人之劍何如？」曰：「庶人之劍，蓬頭突鬢垂冠，曼胡之纓，短後之衣，瞋目而語難。相擊於前，

上斬頸領，下決肝肺。此庶人之劍，無異於鬥雞，一旦命已絕矣，無所用於國事。今大王有天子之位而好

庶人之劍，臣竊為大王薄之。」

ONCE RELEASED FROM ITS SCABBARD, EAST AND WEST PAY HOMAGE TO IT, AND NORTH AND SOUTH HOLD IT IN AWE. SO IT IS CALLED THE NOBLEMAN'S SWORD.

AND THE COMMONER'S SWORD?

THE COMMONER'S SWORD HAS MESSY HAIR, A RASPY VOICE, AND EYES THAT BELONG ON A DEAD FISH.

DRAWN FROM ITS SHEATH, IT SEEKS TO CHOP OFF THE ENEMY'S HEAD AND CUT OUT HIS HEART. THE WARRIOR WHO USES THIS SWORD ISN'T MUCH DIFFERENT FROM A FIGHTING COCK. AS SOON AS HE IS DEAD, HIS CONTRIBUTIONS TO THE COUNTRY HAVE ENDED.

UNFORTUNATELY, YOUR MAJESTY PREFERS THE COMMONER'S SWORD.

王乃牽而上殿。宰人上食，王三環之。莊子曰：「大王安坐定氣，劍事已畢奏矣。」於是文王不出宮三月，劍士皆服斃其處也。

THE SWORD FIGHTING IS OVER. YOU GUYS CAN GO NOW.

OH MY. OH MY. OH MY...

YOUR MAJESTY, RELAX. THE SWORD FIGHTING IS OVER. MY JOB IS DONE. MAY I TAKE MY LEAVE?

YES, OF COURSE

THANK YOU, ZHUANGZI, FOR POINTING OUT MY IGNORANCE.

THE KING RETIRED TO THE PALACE AND DIDN'T COME OUT FOR THREE MONTHS. AND HE NEVER MENTIONED SWORD FIGHTING AGAIN. HIS FIGHTERS WERE SO UPSET AT BEING IGNORED THAT THEY ALL ENDED UP COMMITTING SUICIDE.

THERE ARE MANY DANGEROUS THINGS BESIDES SWORD FIGHTING—FAME, SEX, MONEY, POWER, ETC. THEY CAN ALL INFLICT HARM AND AREN'T WORTH DWELLING ON.

孔子遊乎緇帷之林，休坐乎杏壇之上。弟子讀書，孔子弦歌鼓琴，奏曲未半。有漁父者，下船而來，鬚眉交白，被髮揄袂，行原以上，距陸而止，左手據膝，右手持頤以聽。曲終而招子貢、子路，二人俱對。客指孔子曰：「彼何為者也？」子路對曰：「魯之君子也。」客問其族。子路對曰：「族孔氏。」客曰：「孔氏者何治也？」子路未應，子貢對曰：「孔氏者，性服忠信，身行仁義，飾禮樂，選人倫，上以忠於世主，下以化於齊民，將以利天下。此孔氏之所治也。」又問曰：「有土之君與？」子貢曰：「非也。」「侯王之佐與？」子貢曰：「非也。」

CONFUCIUS IN THE BLACK FOREST

ONE DAY, CONFUCIUS AND HIS FOLLOWERS WERE RELAXING ON THE EDGE OF A DARK FOREST. CONFUCIUS SAT ON A ROCK SINGING AND STRUMMING THE ZITHER, WHILE HIS FOLLOWERS LOUNGED NEARBY STUDYING.

WHO'S THAT SINGING?

HE'S A GENTLEMAN FROM LU.

WHAT'S HIS NAME?

HIS NAME IS CONFUCIUS.

AND WHAT DOES THIS CONFUCIUS DO?

HE TEACHES PEOPLE ABOUT BENEVOLENCE AND RIGHTEOUSNESS, RITUALS AND MUSIC. HIS SINCERE TEACHINGS CONVERT THE MASSES TO GOODNESS AND BRING PEACE TO THE WHOLE LAND.

THEN, HE IS A LANDED GENTLEMAN?

NO, HE'S NOT.

NO, HE'S NOT.

THEN, HE IS THE MINISTER OF A NOBLEMAN?

THEN IT'S TOO BAD HE WORKS SO HARD. IF HE KEEPS ON LIKE THIS, HE'LL ONLY GROW FURTHER AND FURTHER FROM THE DAO!

HA HA HA!

UPON HEARING WHAT THE FISHERMAN SAID...

THAT FISHERMAN IS SO WISE!

WAIT A MINUTE!

YES?

HEARING WHAT YOU JUST SAID, IT SEEMS THAT YOU MAY HAVE MORE TO SAY. IF YOU PLEASE, I WOULD LIKE TO LISTEN.

LET'S TAKE A LOOK AT THE EIGHT SHORTCOMINGS AND FOUR FAILINGS.

TO SERVE THOSE YOU SHOULDN'T IS CALLED: "**HANGING ON.**"

TO HEEDLESSLY RECOMMEND SOMEONE IS CALLED: "**PUFFERY.**"

TO PERSUADE THROUGH MEANINGLESS SPEECH IS CALLED: "**INVEIGLING.**"

TO COMPLIMENT WITH LITTLE REGARD FOR RIGHT OR WRONG IS CALLED: "**FLATTERY.**"

TO ENJOY DISCUSSING THE FAULTS OF OTHERS IS CALLED: "**DISPARAGEMENT.**"

TO BREAK OFF RELATIONS WITH FRIENDS AND FAMILY IS CALLED: "**VILLAINY.**"

TO PRAISE DUPLICITY IN ORDER TO DEFEAT AN OPPONENT IS CALLED: "**DEPRAVITY.**"

TO TAKE WHAT YOU WANT WITHOUT REGARD FOR RIGHT OR WRONG WHILE PRESENTING A FALSE APPEARANCE IS CALLED "**DEVIOUSNESS.**"

客乃笑而還，行言曰：「仁則仁矣，恐不免其身，苦心勞形以危其真。嗚呼，遠哉其分於道也！」子貢還，報孔子。孔子推琴而起曰：「其聖人與！」乃下求之，至於澤畔，方將杖拏而引其船，顧見孔子，還鄉而立。孔子反走，再拜而進。客曰：「子將何求？」孔子曰：……客曰：「且人有八疵，事有四患，不可不察也。非其事而事之，謂之摠；莫之顧而進之，謂之佞；希意導言，謂之諂；不擇是非而言，謂之諛；好言人之惡，謂之讒；析交離親，謂之賊；稱譽詐偽以敗惡人，謂之慝；不擇善否，兩容頗適，偷拔其所欲，謂之險。

221

此八疵者，外以亂人，內以傷身，君子不友，明君不臣。所謂四患者：好經大事，變更易常，以挂功名，謂之叨；專知擅事，侵人自用，謂之貪；見過不更，聞諫愈甚，謂之很；人同於己則可，不同於己，雖善不善，謂之矜。此四患也。能去八疵，無行四患，而始可教已。」孔子愀然而歎，再拜。

EXTENDED OUTWARD, THESE EIGHT SHORTCOMINGS WILL WREAK HAVOC ON OTHER PEOPLE, AND DIRECTED INWARD, THEY WILL DO GREAT HARM TO THE REAL SELF. THEY ARE THINGS WISE PEOPLE DO NOT APPROACH.

AND WHAT ARE THE FOUR FAILINGS?

TO SEEK FAME AND FORTUNE THROUGH GREAT DEEDS, NO MATTER HOW DISRUPTIVE, IS CALLED "CUPIDITY."

TO ACT WITH RECKLESS DISREGARD FOR OTHERS, SELFISHLY CARRYING OUT YOUR OWN PLANS, IS CALLED "AVARICE."

TO SEE YOUR OWN MISTAKES BUT NOT CHANGE, TO HEAR OTHER PEOPLE'S GOOD ADVICE BUT NOT ACT ON IT IS CALLED "DEFIANCE."

TO CALL RIGHT THOSE OPINIONS IN AGREEMENT WITH YOURS AND CALL WRONG THOSE OPINIONS NOT IN AGREEMENT WITH YOURS WITHOUT REGARD TO WHETHER THE OPINIONS ARE TRULY RIGHT OR WRONG IS CALLED "ARROGANCE."

IT'S DIFFICULT TO TALK ABOUT THE DAO WITH ONE WHO POSSESSES THESE FOUR FAILINGS.

IF YOU WANT TO ATTAIN GREAT WISDOM, DON'T BE GUILTY OF THE EIGHT SHORTCOMINGS: HANGING ON, PUFFERY, INVEIGLING, FLATTERY, DISPARAGEMENT, VILLAINY, DEPRAVITY, AND DEVIOUSNESS. AND DON'T BE CAUGHT WITH THE FOUR FAILINGS: CUPIDITY, AVARICE, DEFIANCE, AND ARROGANCE. THESE EIGHT SHORTCOMINGS AND FOUR FAILINGS ARE THE MISTAKES PEOPLE MOST OFTEN COMMIT.

CONFUCIUS'S FACE TURNED PALE, AND HE BOWED THREE TIMES BEFORE DEPARTING.

人有…惡跡而去之走者，舉足愈數而跡愈多，…自以為尚遲，疾走不休，絕力而死。不知…處靜以息跡，愚亦甚矣！

223

愚亦甚矣！

人有畏影……而去之走者，……走愈疾而影不離身，自以為尚遲，疾走不休，絕力而死。不知處陰以休影，……

THE MAN WHO HATED HIS SHADOW

ONCE THERE WAS A MAN WHO HATED HIS OWN SHADOW.

I HATE YOU!
I HATE YOU!
I HATE YOU!

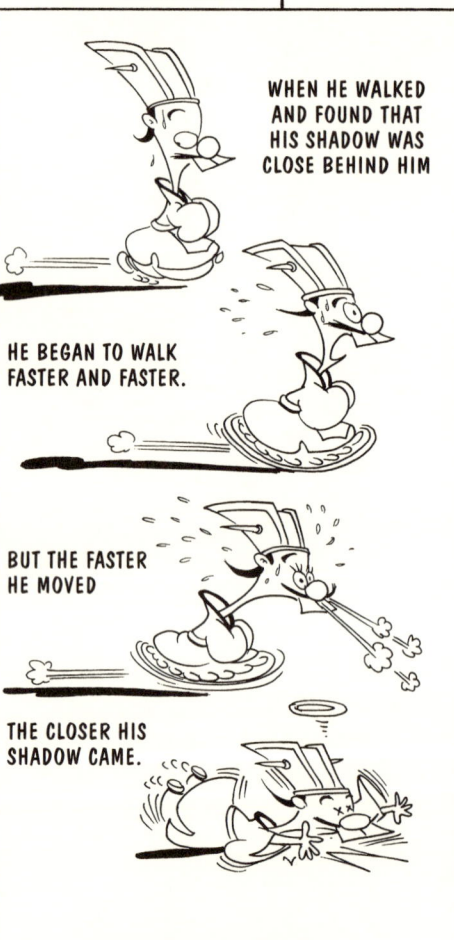

WHEN HE WALKED AND FOUND THAT HIS SHADOW WAS CLOSE BEHIND HIM

HE BEGAN TO WALK FASTER AND FASTER.

BUT THE FASTER HE MOVED

THE CLOSER HIS SHADOW CAME.

SO HE RAN LIKE A MADMAN ... AND IN THE END, HE DROPPED DEAD.

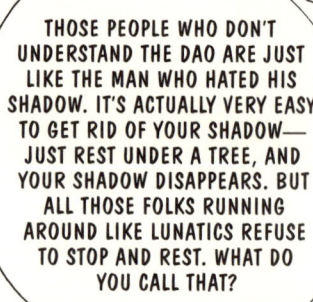

THOSE PEOPLE WHO DON'T UNDERSTAND THE DAO ARE JUST LIKE THE MAN WHO HATED HIS SHADOW. IT'S ACTUALLY VERY EASY TO GET RID OF YOUR SHADOW— JUST REST UNDER A TREE, AND YOUR SHADOW DISAPPEARS. BUT ALL THOSE FOLKS RUNNING AROUND LIKE LUNATICS REFUSE TO STOP AND REST. WHAT DO YOU CALL THAT?

CHAPTER 32
Lie Yukou

巧者勞而知者憂，無能者無所求，飽食而遨遊，汎若不繫之舟，虛而遨遊者也。

226

朱泙漫學屠龍於支離益，單千金之家，三年技成而無所用其巧。

THE DRAGONSLAYER

ZHUPING MAN WAS AN AVID SWORDFIGHTER

ONE DAY, IN HOPES OF STUDYING THE ART OF DRAGONSLAYING, HE WENT TO SEE ZHILI YI.

AFTER STUDYING FOR THREE YEARS AND SPENDING ONE THOUSAND GOLD PIECES OF THE FAMILY SAVINGS,

HEE HEE!

HE FINALLY GRADUATED AND DESCENDED THE MOUNTAIN

CHAPTER 32
LIE YUKOU

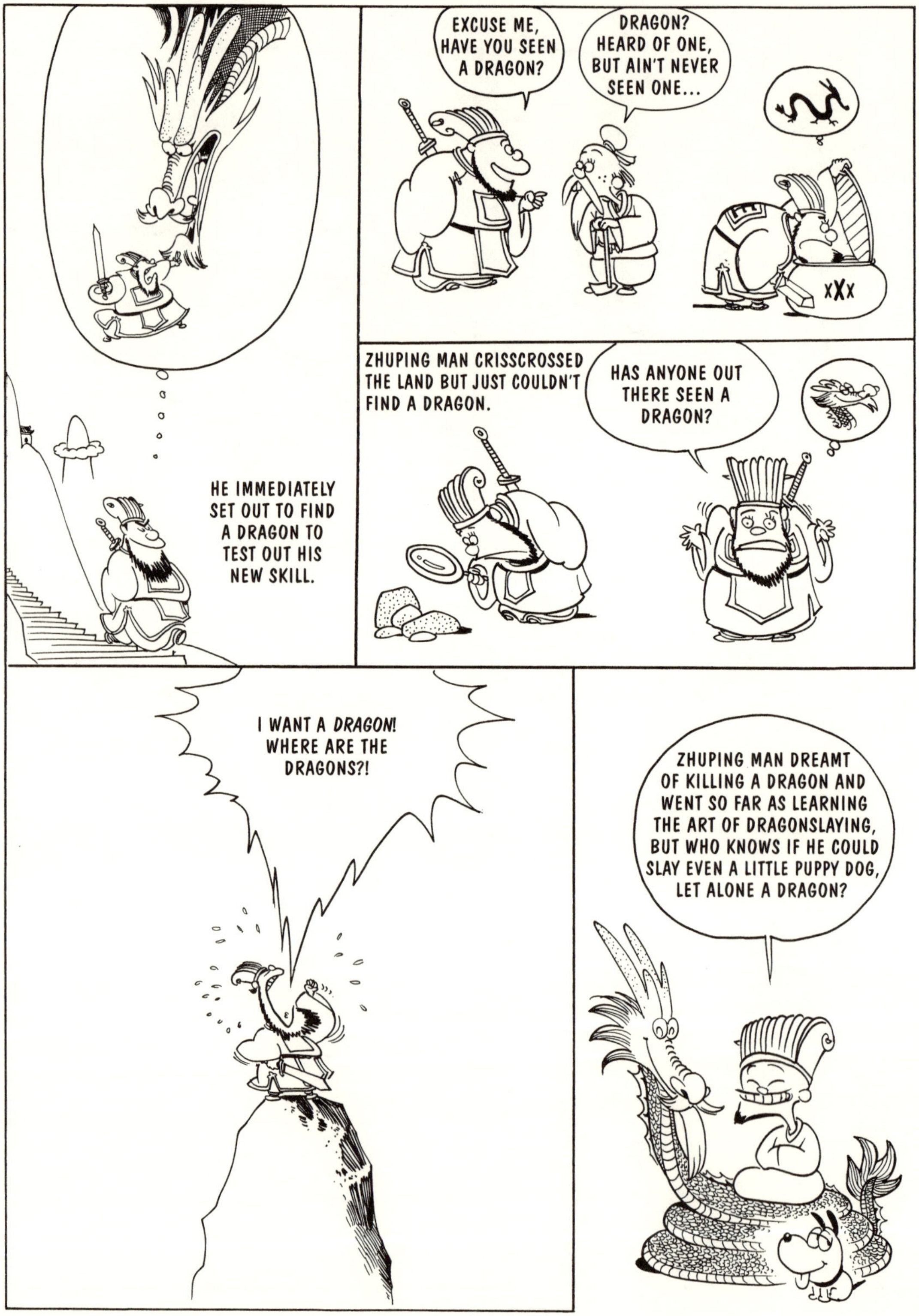
HE IMMEDIATELY SET OUT TO FIND A DRAGON TO TEST OUT HIS NEW SKILL.
EXCUSE ME, HAVE YOU SEEN A DRAGON?
DRAGON? HEARD OF ONE, BUT AIN'T NEVER SEEN ONE...
XXX
ZHUPING MAN CRISSCROSSED THE LAND BUT JUST COULDN'T FIND A DRAGON.
HAS ANYONE OUT THERE SEEN A DRAGON?
I WANT A *DRAGON*! WHERE ARE THE DRAGONS?!
ZHUPING MAN DREAMT OF KILLING A DRAGON AND WENT SO FAR AS LEARNING THE ART OF DRAGONSLAYING, BUT WHO KNOWS IF HE COULD SLAY EVEN A LITTLE PUPPY DOG, LET ALONE A DRAGON?

THE MAN WHO PURSUED PROFIT

FAME FORTUNE

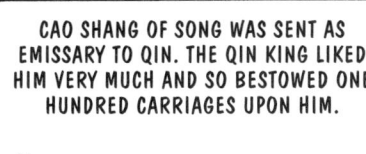

CAO SHANG OF SONG WAS SENT AS EMISSARY TO QIN. THE QIN KING LIKED HIM VERY MUCH AND SO BESTOWED ONE HUNDRED CARRIAGES UPON HIM.

I'M NOT ANY GOOD AT LIVING IN RUN-DOWN ALLEYS, WEAVING SANDALS FOR A LIVING, OR GOING HUNGRY. MY SPECIALTY IS CAJOLING A HUNDRED CARRIAGES FROM A TEN-THOUSAND CARRIAGE SOVEREIGN.

WHEN THE KING GETS AN ILLNESS THAT NEEDS TO BE CURED, HE GIVES A CARRIAGE TO THE PERSON WHO CAN CURE HIM...

TO THE PERSON WHO LICKS HIS BOILS, HE GIVES FIVE CARRIAGES. THE MORE DEMEANING THE TASK, THE GREATER THE NUMBER OF CARRIAGES.

WHAT DESPICABLE THING DID YOU DO TO GET SO MANY CARRIAGES?

PEOPLE OFTEN GO AGAINST THEIR OWN NATURE AND DO DEMEANING AND DESPICABLE THINGS IN PURSUIT OF PROFIT AND STATUS. A GENTLEMAN IS EASYGOING AND HIGH-MINDED. THERE ARE THINGS HE WILL DO, AND THERE ARE THINGS HE WON'T DO.

宋人有曹商者，為宋王使秦。其往也，得車數乘，王悅之，益車百乘。反於宋，見莊子曰：「夫處窮閭阨巷，困窘織屨，槁項黃馘者，商之所短也；一悟萬乘之主而從車百乘者，商之所長也。」莊子曰：「秦王有病召醫，破癰潰痤者得車一乘，舐痔者得車五乘，所治愈下，得車愈多。子豈治其痔邪，何得車之多也？子行矣！」

229

CHAPTER 32
LIE YUKOU

使驪龍而寤，子尚奚微之有哉！』

金之珠。其父謂其子曰：『取石來鍛之！夫千金之珠，必在九重之淵而驪龍頷下，子能得珠者，必遭其睡也。

人有見宋王者，錫車十乘，以其十乘驕稚莊子。莊子曰：『河上有家貧恃緯蕭而食者，其子沒於淵，得千

SHATTERING THE DRAGONPEARL

ONE DAY, A MAN WENT TO ADVISE THE SONG KING.

HA HA HA! WELL SAID! GIVE THIS MAN TEN CHARIOTS.

HEY, ZHUANGZI, LOOK!

HEY, DAD, LOOK!

ONCE THERE WAS A POOR MAN WHO LIVED BY THE EDGE OF THE YELLOW RIVER, AND ONE DAY, HIS SON DOVE DEEP DOWN IN THE RIVER AND CAME UP WITH A GIANT PEARL. HE HANDED THE PEARL TO HIS FATHER, WHO ABRUPTLY SAID, "I DON'T WANT IT!" AND SHATTERED IT AGAINST THE FLOOR.

THAT PEARL HAD TO HAVE BEEN TAKEN FROM THE DARKEST DEPTHS OF THE RIVER BOTTOM, WHERE THE BLACK DRAGON LIVES. YOU WERE ABLE TO GET IT BECAUSE THE DRAGON HAPPENED TO BE SLEEPING AT THE TIME, BUT WHAT IF HE HAD WOKEN UP? WOULD YOU HAVE MADE IT BACK ALIVE?

WHY DID YOU DO THAT?

230

今宋國之深，非直九重之淵也；宋王之猛，非直驪龍也；子能得車者，必遭其睡也。使宋王而寤，子為韲粉夫！」

231

或聘於莊子。莊子應其使曰：「子見夫犧牛乎？衣以文繡，食以芻菽，及其牽而入於太廟，雖欲為孤犢，其可得乎！」

莊子將死，弟子欲厚葬之。莊子曰：「吾以天地為棺槨，以日月為連璧，星辰為珠璣，萬物為齎送。吾葬具豈不備邪？何以加此！」弟子曰：「吾恐烏鳶之食夫子也。」莊子曰：「在上為烏鳶食，在下為螻蟻食，奪彼與此，何其偏也！」

233

Pronunciation Index

There are different systems of Romanization of Chinese words, but in all of these systems the sounds of the letters used do not necessarily correspond to those sounds which we are accustomed to using in English (for instance, would you have guessed that zh is pronounced like j as in "jelly"—not as in "je ne sais quoi"?). Of course, these systems can be learned, but to save some time and effort for the reader who is not a student of Chinese, we have provided the following pronunciation guide. The Chinese words appear on the left as they do in the text and are followed by their pronunciations. Just sound out the pronunciations as you would sound out any English word, and you will be quite close to the proper Mandarin Chinese pronunciation.

In addition, Chinese philosophical terms have been defined, and page numbers have been provided where every glossed term appears in the book.

NOTES

–dz is a combination of d and z in one sound, without the ee sound at the end; so it sounds kind of like a bee in flight with a slight d sound at the beginning.

–zh is pronounced like the j in "jelly" and not like the j in "je ne sais quoi."